Gerald McDermott and YOU

Gerald McDermott and YOU

Jon C. Stott

Foreword and Illustrations by Gerald McDermott

The Author and YOU

LIBRARIES
UNLIMITED
A Member of the Greenwood Publishing Group

Westport, Connecticut • London

British Library Cataloguing in Publication Data is available.

Copyright © 2004 by Jon C. Stott and Gerald McDermott

All rights reserved. No portion of this book may be reproduced, by any process or technique, without the express written consent of the publisher.

ISBN: 1-59158-175-3

First published in 2004

Libraries Unlimited, 88 Post Road West, Westport, CT 06881
A member of the Greenwood Publishing Group, Inc.
www.lu.com

Printed in the United States of America

The paper used in this book complies with the Permanent Paper Standard issued by the National Information Standards Organization (Z39.48-1984)

10 9 8 7 6 5 4 3 2 1

To
Gerald McDermott, author
Marie Whalen, teacher and principal
Sophie Caroline and Gillian Jacqueline, young readers and granddaughters
this book is dedicated

Contents

Preface   ix
Gerald McDermott

Series Foreword   xi
Sharon Coatney and Sharron McElmeel

Introduction   xiii

The Author: Gerald McDermott—A Life in Story   1

The Stories and You   9

- Eleven stories discussed with engagement and extension ideas
  Anansi the Spider   13
  Arrow to the Sun   21
  The Stonecutter   31
  Papagayo the Mischief Maker   39
  Daniel O'Rourke   47
  Zomo the Rabbit   55
  Raven   63
  Coyote   71
  Musicians of the Sun   77
  Jabutí the Tortoise   85
  Creation   91

Other McDermott Books Briefly Considered   99

- Six stories briefly discussed
  The Magic Tree   99
  The Voyage of Osiris   99
  The Knight of the Lion   100
  Sunflight   101
  Daughter of Earth   102
  Tim O'Toole and the Wee Folk   102

Bibliographies of Gerald McDermott's Works   105

An Index of Authors, Artists, and Titles   107

Preface

When I first set out on my artist's journey, I imagined the path I was to follow in a linear way, much like the "Rainbow Trail" that runs through the pages of *Arrow to the Sun*. Now, after many decades trodding this path, is seems to me it is more like the double spiral I portrayed in *Creation*, a path that begins at the center of my existence, spirals outward to the edges of the cosmos, then coils inward to replenish my soul with newly discovered energies.

Mythology and folklore have been the foundation for most of my creative work, in films and in books. My goal has been to render these ancient tales in ways that were vital and engaging. Equally important was to bring viewers and readers along on the journey with me, not simply as passive observers, but challenging them to bring the same degree of curiosity and passion to the reading of the book as I did to the writing and drawing.

I want my readers to see the world in a fresh and imaginative way, to grow in knowledge and experience of many different cultures, to internalize the message of the myths, to understand that these ancient themes are alive and moving within us.

Creating the books has been for me a visceral process. It begins at the moment I choose a story . . . or rather at the moment a story "chooses" me. These tales resonate with deep psychological truths and profound human emotions that transcend culture and time. Although I may not understand fully why a particular story draws me in, I try to remain open to its message. With the perspective of time, I can see clearly that the emotional core of each story was important to me at that moment on the path of life. I continue to rely on that instinct and trust it to carry me through the months of research, writing, and painting required to bring the work to completion.

What eventually emerges as a published work, "public" in the largest sense, begins as a deeply private moment. When I have internalized the arc of the story, understood its characters and the drama of the tale, I walk around my studio declaiming the tale, telling myself the story over and over again, listening to the rhythms of my own voice. The act of reciting out loud allows the sound to vibrate in my diaphragm, to rise up from a cellular level and become a living presence, to emerge as spoken word.

Because these stories spring from oral tradition, I want my rendition to stand as an oral telling even if no one ever sees my words in print or looks at my illustrations. The oral telling has to carry the meaning and drama of the story. By the time I sit down and put pencil to paper, the story is already written and, in effect, I am simply taking dictation.

The creation of the artwork is physically involving, too. I stand, rather than sit, in front of my drawing board, first sketching with pencil and pastel, actively rubbing out, erasing, tearing paper sketches apart and reassembling them with tape and glue. Then I transfer those images to a larger surface and begin working in color, using gouache and fabric paint, then pastels and colored pencils to darken, shade, and modulate my illustrations. I strive to animate my characters in two dimensions, to surprise and delight the eye, to astonish with a page turn, to avoid the visual cliché, the graphic convention. Above all, I avoid answering all the visual questions and use open-ended, stylized imagery so that the reader can see in abstract shapes and forms new worlds of possibilities that lie behind or beyond the image. My main goal is to keep open a pathway to the reader's imagination and be the messenger between the world of everyday and the realm of the imagination.

The myths embody larger truths about life and express them through symbol and metaphor. Though these stories may spring from a time and place that is remote, they dramatize common human concerns that link us with others and reveal in "others" ourselves.

Whether they are hero tales or symbolic journeys toward the light of consciousness or trickster tales masquerading as protoscience, they sound themes of friendship and betrayal, compassion and spiritual rebirth. These themes run through the stories like an underground stream that bubbles up to the surface of consciousness, and they lead ultimately to what my friend and mentor Joseph Campbell called "a poetic revelation of the mystery of that which is now and forever and within your own being."

Grateful acknowledgments to Sharon Coatney, who first suggested this book, and to Jon Stott, who is the most articulate, passionate, and perceptive guide to my work I could have hoped for.

Gerald McDermott
www.geraldmcdermott.com

Series Foreword

Have you ever wanted to sit down and talk with the author of a beloved story? Have you ever wanted to find out more? Good authors are like good friends. They touch our hearts and minds. They make us wonder, and want to learn.

When young readers become engaged with a story, they invariably ask questions.

- Why is Gerald McDermott so fascinated with myths and legends? How did he locate and choose which stories he wished to retell? How do the images in his books convey the culture represented in the story while still retaining his own artistic vision?
- Did Alma Flor Ada know the people that we meet in her stories? Where does she come from? Why does she write in Spanish and English?
- Can Toni Buzzeo tell us how much of the *Sea Chest* is legend and what part is fact? What character does she like best: the Dawdle Ducking, Papa Loon? How does she get her ideas?

As teachers and librarians, we know that the moment children begin asking questions, we are presented with a wonderful opportunity. In response, we may hold discussions or create learning activities. Yet, answers to some questions are hard to come by. After all, our students and we cannot just sit down and talk with the authors we love and admire. But wouldn't it be great if we could?

Libraries Unlimited has developed *The Author and YOU* series to give you the next best thing to a real life visit with your favorite children's authors and illustrators. In these books, you'll hear from authors and illustrators as they reflect on their work and explain to YOU, the reader, what they really had in mind. You'll find answers to some of the questions you and your students might ask, and to some you never thought to ask.

Just as each author or illustrator is a unique individual, so will his or her conversation with YOU be unique and individual. There is no formula, no pre-designed structure. We've simply asked the authors or illustrators to discuss the things they each think are important or interesting about themselves and their books—and to share their comments with YOU.

Some authors will provide actual ideas and plans for you to use in sharing books with young readers. Others will share ideas that will help you generate your own ideas and connections to their work. In some cases the author writes the book in collaboration with another. In others, it is a private reflection; but in all cases you'll discover some fascinating information and come away with valuable insights.

It is our hope that by giving you these special messages from authors and illustrators, *The Author and YOU* series will increase your joy and understanding of literature—and in turn, will help YOU motivate young readers, surround them with literacy and literacy activities, and share the joy of understanding.

Sharon Coatney
Sharron McElmeel

Introduction

I first encountered the works of Gerald McDermott in 1974 when I received a review copy of *Arrow to the Sun*. I quickly recognized that it treated a theme frequently found in children's literature: a different, rejected child performed actions that led to his being accepted, and often acclaimed, by peers who had earlier treated him so badly. I also recognized that it was set in the Southwest, among the Pueblo peoples. However, beyond the fact that these Native Americans lived in distinctive villages set in an arid landscape, I knew little about their lives and culture.

Over the next few years, I read McDermott's other picture books, recognizing his interest in a variety of cultures and their art styles, but I generally thought and taught about the books according to the ways they resembled stories from the Western tradition. Then, in 1979, at a Children's Literature Association conference in Toronto, I met and conducted a lengthy interview with the author. Our conversation touched on basic biographical items—his childhood interests and training in the fine arts—but focused on two topics: his interactions with Joseph Campbell, the renowned scholar of world mythologies, and his extensive research into not only the artistic styles but also the cultural values and spiritual beliefs of the people whose stories he had adapted into picture book form.

A few months after this meeting, I was invited to speak at a teachers' conference and decided to talk about *Arrow to the Sun*, showing members of the audience how, by acquiring a fuller sense of the cultural backgrounds of the story, they could enhance their presentations of the book and their young audiences' responses to it. In preparation, I read several books about the artistic styles, religious ceremonies, and daily life of the Pueblo nations of western New Mexico and eastern Arizona and began to see the events, characters, and visual details of the picture book in a new light. I also read Campbell's *The Hero with a Thousand Faces*, finding in the study discussions that cast light on the psychological aspects of the Boy's journey in *Arrow to the Sun* and that helped me to see parallels between McDermott's book, various Arthurian legends, the Blackfoot myth about Scarface, and such recent movies as *Superman* and *Star Wars*.

My meeting with Gerald McDermott, my background research, and my subsequent reexamination of *Arrow to the Sun* had two immediate results. They influenced my presentations of the book to groups of first and sixth graders in Edmonton, Canada, and these, in turn, influenced my address to the teachers.

Moreover, these experiences set a pattern that has continued over a quarter of a century. Gerald McDermott and I have met at frequent intervals since our introduction in 1979. Our conversations have ranged widely—his current work; the place that his art and storytelling occupies in his life; his work with schoolchildren; reflections on literature, art, and the state of the world. The appearance of each of his new books has led me to the story's sources and its cultural roots.

My studies have formed the basis of a number of essays and book chapters, most dealing with his treatment of North American native myths and legends. I continued to integrate McDermott's books into literature programs I was developing in Canada and the United States. And many of these ideas were incorporated with those of my friend and colleague Christine Doyle in a study guide we published in 1989 for Book Wise, Incorporated.

The present book marks a bringing together of these activities—conversations, academic studies, presentations to teachers' groups, and work with elementary and junior high school readers. Part One, "The Author," traces Gerald McDermott's career, interspersing his comments with my analysis and commentary on developing themes and styles of his works. Part Two, "The Stories and You," focuses on eleven of the most important of his picture books. A brief analysis of each story is followed by the author's own commentary on it. Extensive suggestions are then given for presenting the story to children and relating it to the rest of the author's books as well as to similar stories by other writers and artists.

An undertaking such as this, even though it bears one author's name on the title page, is not achieved without a tremendous amount of encouragement and assistance from many individuals. To Sharon Coatney of Libraries Unlimited goes my gratitude for inviting me to engage in this project, for exercising so much patience with me during the planning, writing, and revising stages, and for gently offering valuable suggestions that have made this a better project. To colleagues, journal editors, and conference organizers who have indulged me in my efforts to understand and talk about the works of Gerald McDermott go my thanks. I wish particularly to thank Jacque Shrader of Annapolis, Maryland, and Christine Doyle of Central Connecticut State University, who shared with me their very creative ways of engaging children with McDermott's works. And finally, I owe a debt of gratitude to the teachers and students in many, many schools in two countries. They have generously allowed me into their classrooms and have instructed and enlightened me more than I have them.

Finally, I wish to acknowledge the importance of the four people whose names appear on the dedication page. Gerald McDermott has, over the years, become a very good friend. It was he who suggested that I be the author for a book about his stories and he has provided input and encouragement throughout the process. Marie Whalen, a principal in the Edmonton Catholic School District first invited me to work with her students and teachers in 1982. Twenty-two years later, the classrooms in her schools are still open to me. Sophie Caroline and Gillian Jacqueline, my first grandchildren, are learning, on the knees of their father, mother, and grandfather, the joys of engaging with picture books, thus continuing a family tradition that goes back at least five generations.

An artist, a school teacher and principal, young children—they symbolize the people involved in the world of children's books, and their influence on this book is implicit on every page. I thank them for the inspiration they have provided; I treasure their friendships.

Gerald McDermott and YOU

The Author

Gerald McDermott— A Life in Story

"THE CHILD IS FATHER OF THE MAN"

Two centuries ago, the English poet William Wordsworth wrote this paradoxical statement to emphasize how important childhood experiences were in determining the characters and lives of adults. This is certainly the case for Gerald McDermott, who, by the time he'd graduated from high school had acquired a grounding in literature, drama, music, dance, and painting that would lay the foundation for his achievements, first as a filmmaker and then as a major author of children's books.

McDermott had the great good fortune to have parents who loved the arts and encouraged and supported his talents. He remembers his mother and father reading to him from a collection of folk and fairy tales called *My Book House.* "Once I learned to read, it wouldn't be uncommon to find the three of us sitting in the living room, my father in his easy chair, my mother on the sofa, and me curled up on the floor, reading. We were each absorbed in our own book, but there was a real sense of togetherness and a shared experience. At one time, my father decided he'd supplement his modest paycheck by selling sets of Child Craft books door to door. He only sold one set—to us. But I read and reread the stories in it. Looking back, I can see that those books provided my entry into the worlds of mythology and folklore. In fact, the story of *The Stonecutter*, my first film, came from one of the collections."

Gerald didn't just listen to stories and read. Before he started school, he'd shown such an interest in sketching and painting that his parents enrolled him in Saturday morning classes at his hometown's great museum, the Detroit Institute of Arts. "I went there every Saturday for ten years. We'd have a morning's instruction on art basics: drawing shapes, working with colors. Then, in the afternoons before our families came to pick us up, we'd be encouraged to wander through the collection and sketch from the various works. A great many were about mythological subjects. I think that was another reason I was drawn to myth when I began to make films and, later, books."

There were other rich artistic experiences. In the two years before his voice broke, he was an actor in "Storyland," a weekly radio show in Detroit. "I learned about how to introduce sound effects and music into a narrative. At one point, my father, who worked for Michigan Bell, brought home a wire recorder and I used it to create my own programs—writing, doing the voices, mixing music and sound. These experiences really helped me when I began making animated films."

At the time, he also studied ballet and music, learning stylized movement and formal musical patterns, both of which had, over centuries, been vehicles for representing traditional folk tales and myths. "Music has been important to me since childhood; it is a powerful catalyst to my imagination," McDermott has said. These two arts became important elements of McDermott's films, and in his books they are important for the narratives. In many ways, the challenge of creating pictures books has been, for him, to find effective means of translating movement and sound to the still, silent page.

The young artist became a student at Cass Tech, a public high school in Detroit noted for its excellent arts programs. He received rigorous, highly structured training that gave formal focus to the various artistic experiences he had enjoyed to that point. Based on the German Bauhaus principle that form followed function, it would help McDermott to make all aspects of his art work toward achieving its intellectual, aesthetic, and emotional purposes. Art was not to be merely decorative, but to be communicative—in a word, functional. It was during this time that he began to employ the principles he was learning to animated films.

All through his elementary and high school years, he continued a habit he'd developed first as a youngster, when he began sketching figures on the margins of his family's Yellow Pages directory, then flipping the pages to animate them. He doodled, "thinking visually aloud," articulating graphically the ideas that interested him.

PORTRAIT OF THE ARTIST AS A YOUNG MAN

In 1959, McDermott was awarded a National Scholastic Scholarship and left Detroit for New York City to attend Pratt Institute. He spent over a decade in New York, where he not only continued his studies but also worked as a television graphic designer and produced four of his own animated films, met one of the foremost twentieth-century scholars of mythology, and received an invitation to turn his animated adaptations of traditional tales into children's books. He also spent a summer traveling in Europe, meeting and studying with distinguished filmmakers in England, France, and Yugoslavia. It is safe to say that in this decade, the interests, talents, and training of his childhood and high school years came into focus and his understanding of the meaning and purpose of his art deepened.

In Paris, he walked into the office of Henri Langlois, the founder of the Cinémathèque Française, and presented his one animated film. Langlois, in turn, introduced him to the Russian-émigré artist and filmmaker Alexander Alexieff. McDermott was profoundly impressed by Alexieff's stylized animation, his lifestyle, and his devotion to his art. The young artist came away from that encounter with a determination to pursue his own artistic vision to the exclusion of all other work.

McDermott graduated from Pratt in 1964 with a Bachelor of Fine Arts. But it is as much what he didn't study at Pratt as what he did that helped him to become an acclaimed visual and verbal reteller of myths, legends, and folktales. Because Pratt did not offer film studies, which he had become interested in while at Cass Tech, he decided to create an animated film as a summer project and returned to *The Stonecutter*, the Japanese story he'd loved as a child. Work on the ten-minute film involved intense and extensive research into the culture and customs of the story's originators, along with a search for music that would express the emotions and abstract ideas that couldn't be effectively communicated visually or verbally.

He also learned a great deal when he withdrew from his studies during the 1962–1963 school year to work as the first graphic designer at WNET (Channel 13), New York's fledgling public television station. He developed visual designs to symbolize or embody the ideas of programs to be broadcast. The stylized owl logo he created to represent the station remained popular for many years and was, in many ways, a forerunner of the symbols that would identify characters in his stories.

After graduating and just as he had begun work on his second film, *Sunflight/The Flight of Icarus*, a retelling of a well-known Greek legend, McDermott had one of the most important encounters of his professional and personal life. "The producer of the film asked me to come into his office to meet a friend," he recalled. "'He's someone you should talk to,' the producer said. So I went in, was introduced and then my friend's guest and I had an hour's conversation. My education on the psychological dimensions of mythology began that day."

The man he met was Joseph Campbell, then a professor at Sarah Lawrence College and one of the foremost authorities on world mythology. He was the author of *The Hero with a Thousand Faces* and *The Masks of God*, highly influential studies of the similarities underlying myths from diverse and geographically widely separated cultures. Campbell, who had studied the works of psychologist Carl Jung, believed that these similarities arose from the fact that the ancient stories embodied basic, universal human concerns. For him, each tale elaborated on the emotional and spiritual journeys made by all people as they searched for their identities, for answers to the questions, "Who am I? Where do I belong?"

"Suddenly," McDermott explained, "thanks to my discussions with Campbell, the stories I'd been fascinated with all my life began to resonate in a new way; I could see deeper levels in them. This had an impact on my illustrations. I began to look for graphic, visual ways to communicate the psychological levels of the stories."

Campbell became a consultant for McDermott's later films. His influence can be seen most fully in *The Magic Tree*, where the idea of a great tree as the center of life plays an important role, and *Arrow to the Sun*, in which the Boy undergoes the solitary journey of initiation that Campbell believed was central to male quest stories. "We met regularly over the years, and he led me to study the works of Jung, Mircea Eliade [a scholar of world religions] and Otto Rank [an analyst of mythology]. The insights I gained from their works had a tremendous influence on my thinking and the books I created."

The film *Sunflight* appeared in 1966, *Anansi the Spider* in 1969, and *The Magic Tree* in 1970. These films traced the failed quest of the central male figures and used culturally relevant art to depict underlying psychological meanings. McDermott was well into his career as a maker of animated films and received awards from such organizations as the Venice Film Festival, the Annecy Film Festival, the American Film Festival, the San Francisco Film Festival, and the Sri Lanka International Film Festival.

BECOMING A CHILDREN'S AUTHOR-ILLUSTRATOR

Shortly after the early showings of *Anansi*, he had another encounter that influenced the direction of his career. George Nicholson, children's book editor at Holt, Rinehart, and Winston, had attended a screening of the film and then had contacted McDermott. He made what was, to the filmmaker, a novel suggestion. Why not turn the animated stories into children's books? McDermott agreed and, between 1970 and 1972, while living in southern France, explored ways of turning stories that had been told through up to six thousand separate animated drawings, with accompanying music, dialogue, and sound effects, into silent, thirty-two-page picture books. *Anansi the Spider*, the first of these, appeared in 1972 and was awarded a Caldecott Honor Book, as a runner-up for the American Library Association's award for the most distinguished picture book of the year. *The Magic Tree* followed in 1973, and *Arrow to the Sun*, in 1974. The latter story, the first McDermott developed simultaneously in both film and book form, was named the winner of the Caldecott Medal.

Arrow to the Sun was the last of McDermott's animated films. The intensity of the labor involved in creating thousands of frames and the complicated production process had become too time-consuming. He decided to turn his attention to retelling myths in book form only. His next two retellings, *The Voyage of Osiris* (1977) and *The Knight of the Lion* (1979), marked a conscious departure from the artistic style of the films and, by extension, of the books based on them. The sharply defined figures and the stylized graphics were replaced by a more fluid style that communicated the sense of physical movement and the theme of inner transformation more effectively on the still page.

The experimentation continued with *Papagayo: The Mischief Maker* (1980), an original story based on the escapades of a popular Brazilian folk character, and *Daughter of Earth* (1984), a retelling of a Roman myth. In the former, one of the first of several trickster tales he would tell, McDermott created clear background colors against which the sharp cut-out figures enacted the drama. In the latter, which along with *The Magic Tree*, *The Knight of the Lion*, and *The Voyage of Osiris* dealt with the intense relationships between men and women, the illustrations imitated the style of Roman fresco art.

During the 1980s, McDermott published two books that paid homage to the storytelling traditions of his Irish ancestors: *Daniel O'Rourke* (1986) and *Tim O'Toole and the Wee Folk* (1990). During this period he also illustrated a number of books written by Marianna Mayer. These collaborations, the only ones of his career, included a series of concept books featuring a family of animals called the Brambleberries and abridged adaptations of *The Adventures of Pinocchio* (1981) and *Aladdin and the Enchanted Lamp* (1985). Not only do the illustrations for the adapted classics depict key characters and important events, they also reflect McDermott's interest in the spiritual and psychological dimensions of the hero's journey.

Beginning in the early 1990s, McDermott began two closely related projects: a series of trickster tales from around the world and two works in which mythological creation stories were paralleled to the creative processes of individuals. *Zomo the Rabbit: A Trickster Tale from West Africa* (1992), *Raven: A Trickster Tale from the Pacific Northwest* (1993), *Coyote: A Trickster Tale from the American Southwest* (1994), and *Jabutí the Tortoise: A Trickster Tale from the Amazon* (2001) recount the adventures and misadventures of well-known folk figures. In them, the main characters' energies are sometimes directed toward constructive and sometimes toward selfish goals. While the central characters frequently succeed, they are sometimes self-defeating, and often, victims. McDermott, who had been fascinated by the antics of tricksters for many years, saw them as humorous examples of individuals whose quests for self-fulfillment and social integration have not always been successful. In retelling the stories, he frequently made use of the stylized graphic techniques of his early works, but with a greater sense of movement, and he incorporated into the books the folk arts of the cultures originating the tales.

Raven, for which McDermott received his second Caldecott Honor Medal, also introduced a theme developed more fully in *Musicians of the Sun* (1997) and *Creation* (2003): the arrival of light and life into a setting of darkness and, sometimes, chaos. Although many of Raven's adventures involve selfish mischief making, he is sometimes depicted as a divine being. In this story, he uses his wits and ability to transform in order to liberate the sun, thus giving the people the daylight they enjoy today. In *Musicians of the Sun*, the character Wind performs a similar role, freeing four musicians from bondage to Sun and bringing them to the world, where their music brings light and joy to people who had labored in darkness. In *Creation*, the artist's most ambitious adaptation to date, the event celebrated is nothing less than the forming of the world and its creatures out of darkness. He has noted that on a parallel level, the artist is similarly a liberator and bringer of light, illuminating the darkness and shaping form and pattern out of what had been fragmented and chaotic.

PICTURE BOOKS AND THE POWER OF MYTH

Unlike many creators of picture books, whose works cover a variety of genres and subjects, realism and fantasy, contemporary and historical, traditional and original stories, McDermott has focused intensely and deeply on a one type of story: traditional narratives of various cultures, tales that had been originally told orally over many generations. These have generally been classified in three categories. Myths, the sacred narratives of a culture, deal with the supernatural beings, the gods, and frequently with their interactions with human beings and the rest of the creation. *Creation, Musicians of the Sun, Arrow to the Sun, Daughter of Earth, Raven,* and *The Voyage of Osiris* are myths. Legends may include supernatural beings but focus on often larger than life mortals, heroic human beings. *The Knight of the Lion, Sunflight,* and *The Magic Tree* are in this category. Folktales frequently involve magic, but they are short, often humorous stories in which the actions of the characters—who are often animals—provide examples of positive and negative behavior and attitude. *The Stonecutter, Anansi the Spider, Papagayo, Daniel O'Rourke, Zomo, Coyote, Tim O'Toole and the Wee Folk,* and *Jabutí* are folktales.

McDermott has frequently commented on the nature of myth, legend, and folklore, pointing out the symbolic elements and the stories' significance in human life. In the preface to his first book, *Anansi the Spider,* he wrote: "Mythology transforms, making the ordinary into the magical. It brings beauty to the ways of man, giving him dignity and expressing his joy in life. Folklore prepares man for adult life. It places him within his culture. With oral traditions, retold through generations, the social group maintains its continuity, handing down its culture." These stories, he noted, are about individuals' quests for self-fulfillment, for self-transformation. "They are about the task of self-creation." The characters in myths and folktales establish their personal and cultural identities. They find out who they are and where they belong. Or, in some cases, because of character flaws, because of behavior that sets them in opposition to their cultural group, they fail. The characters, events, settings, and objects in traditional stories are symbols that embody psychological elements that human beings recognize and relate to and culture-specific values and morals. Responding to these stories, people are discovering guidelines for their own lives.

McDermott has remarked that of the thousands of myths, legends, and folktales he has read, the ones he has retold seem to have chosen him, rather than he them. "They relate to the particular stage I'm at on my journey of life. Because the great myths have emerged from the deepest part of the human consciousness, certain ones will resonate with certain individuals at key times. I've really been guided along my path by these stories. My earlier works focused on individuals defining or failing to define themselves and about personal relationships. Later I needed a lighter, more humorous way of dealing with important themes, and I turned to the trickster stories. In a way, I identified with Zomo the Rabbit. Like him, I felt small and I had to use my wits to survive. Later, when I retold the Raven story, I could feel my artistic energy growing; I was transforming and spreading my wings. Most recently I've been drawn to myths of creation; they've helped me to understand my role as an artist, a creator."

But recreating a story that has been told many times over centuries is not a matter of just simply responding to a story that has called out. After the visceral, emotional, psychological reaction, a great deal of hard work must be undertaken if the artist is to articulate successfully his version of the narrative and its deeper meanings. "Once I've studied different versions of the tale and got a sense of the story's structure and details," McDermott reported, "I walk around talking out loud, saying the story over and over, so that the sentences take on a kind of poetic rhythm and the verbal telling becomes my own. Then I set down the words on paper." Countless hours of editing the written text follow. "Often the final version will be half the length of the one I first wrote down. I work to achieve a lean, spare, evocative text that only says in words what I can't show in pictures."

As the verbal part of the story begins to assume its final form, McDermott carries on extensive research into the culture from which it came, learning not only about costumes, art styles, and the landscape, but also about the people's rituals and the social and religious foundations. Although his initial response is personal, if he is to succeed in retelling it, he must know what it means to the people who originally told it. How would they have envisioned the characters and events? How would they have interpreted these? "One of the important aspects of mythology is its imagery; it's so powerful that it has been a primary way of conjuring up the force of a particular myth. I look for a way to combine my own and traditional people's visual elements in my retelling."

The visual retelling usually begins with a series of thumbnail sketches by which the artist takes tentative steps toward articulating the power and meaning of the story. This is followed with a sequence of drawings that outline what McDermott has referred to as the "arc of the story," its narrative and thematic structure. The final book is quite similar to these sketches. Images are carefully articulated so that they reflect the cultural meanings and the colors chosen that communicate the story's emotional, psychological power. McDermott has commented on the importance of achieving a blend of his modern graphic style and traditional folk art. "The object of my art is not to depict every last detail. The illustrations aren't intended to be realistic. They are intended to evoke a response in the readers, to suggest ways of entering into and experiencing the power of the story, both as it relates to them and to the originating culture. Folk art is particularly good at that."

Neither the words nor the pictures of the completed book tell the story alone. The meaning emerges in part from the dynamic interaction and even tension between them. Sometimes, indeed, words are completely absent from a page or series of pages, and readers must create their own verbal narratives after noticing and responding to the design, color, and details of one or more pictures. Indeed, McDermott believes that one of the functions of storytellers, be they performing in front of a group, telling tales through the sound and movement of animated films, or presenting them by placing words and pictures on the pages of books, is to engage audiences, to make them participants in the creation of meaning.

In talking about his role and responsibility as a writer-artist recreating traditional stories, Gerald McDermott has frequently compared his function to that of a shaman in traditional cultures. The existence of shamans "has grown directly from our archaic need for an interpreter of the magic world obscured by common sight." The shaman, a religious visionary and healer, was able to travel beyond the material, physical world into realms of great spiritual power. When he returned, he communicated his experiences, often through stories. He was able to renew the spiritual, emotional energies of his people through reconnecting them with vital sources. The storyteller is similar: by retelling the most powerful traditional tales in ways that engage people, he also helps to reconnect and regenerate them.

He also keeps the ancient stories alive but infuses them with his own aesthetic, spiritual, and emotional responses and recasts them in ways that make them accessible and relevant to new, changed audiences. "My purpose is to explore and share the evocative qualities of these ancient tales with those still open to the message of myth." And, although he did not initially set out to retell these stories for young audiences, children have turned out to be his natural constituency, for they still possess the imaginative receptivity to the power of myth. The storyteller's goal, he has explained, "is to open the way for the spirit of the young reader to soar."

And people of all ages who have engaged with the picture books of Gerald McDermott will agree that he has fulfilled his mission, has achieved his goal—countless times.

References

Helmer, Dona. "The Inside Story: The Art of Gerald McDermott." *Book Links* (May 1995), 20–25.

Moulton, Priscilla. "Gerald McDermott," in *Newbery and Caldecott Medal Books: 1966–1975*, ed. Lee Kingman. Boston: Hornbook, 1975.

The Stories and You

Two assumptions underlie the following discussions of Gerald McDermott's picture books. First, stories are made up of implicitly significant details arranged into implicitly significant patterns. Second, stories imitate other stories.

Creators of stories select characters, actions, settings, and other details that are important in the development of plots, conflicts, and themes. However, the importance of these components and their arrangements is implicit; that is, authors invite readers to discover why these details are selected and then presented and arranged in the ways they are. Although each story is unique, it bears resemblances to other stories. Not only are tellers and retellers of stories drawing on standard story elements such as conflict, character development, and irony, they are also using recognizable story types or genres, such as the hero's quest or the trickster's misadventures. In addition, authors will return to themes, as well as plot and character types that they have dealt with in their previous stories. Readers, by keeping in mind their understanding of how stories work generally, along with their familiarity with story types and other works by a specific author, will have frameworks that will assist them in their engagement with each new story they consider.

The following introductions and author's discussions for McDermott's stories are intended to present readers with ideas that will facilitate recognition of implicit details and patterns of the books. The engagement and extension activities suggest ways that younger readers can notice and interpret details and patterns and can relate the book being discussed to other McDermott titles and to similar stories by other authors.

One way to facilitate young readers' awareness of relationships among stories is to encourage them to complete a "Family of Stories" chart after reading a story. In the circle at the center of the chart, students write the name of the story they are presently studying. Then, in the circles at the end of the "spokes" radiating from the central circle, they can write the names of stories that share some element with the "central" story (for example, a common culture, a plot resemblance, a character type, a specific type of action). On the spokes, they can signify the aspect the two stories share.

The Family of Stories

For example, if the story in the central circle is *Arrow to the Sun*, one of the outer circles might list *Frederick* (by Leo Lionni) and along the spoke could be written "outcast" (as both Frederick and the Boy are rejected by their peers early in the stories). In another circle might be written *The Legend of Scarface* (Robert San Souci), and on the spoke, "sun journey." After filling out a chart (either individually, in pairs or small groups, or as an entire class), students could discuss the similarities between the pairs of stories more fully and also could discuss differences. In order to strengthen the ability to see relationships between stories, students should complete a "Family of Stories" chart after reading each McDermott story.

To facilitate readers' ability to perceive and explain the implicit significance of details in stories, students studying a group of McDermott stories could keep a "Dictionary of Character and Emotions." After reading a story, students can chose words that best describe the character traits and emotions of the main individuals in the story. Each word could be listed on a page of a notebook of twenty four pages (one page each for the letters *A* to *W* and one for *X-Y-Z.* After the character or emotion word, the character's name can be listed, along with a detail from the story that illustrates the quality. Teachers might wish, before reading a story, to prepare a list of character and emotion words (not all of them applicable to the story) that can be discussed after the reading of the story, but before the students work on their dictionaries. There are two goals for this activity. First, when students discover that characters from different stories can be listed under the same word, they can see how McDermott is interested in certain character types. Second, students can expand their vocabularies and can avoid falling into what one educator has jokingly called the "sad-glad-mad-bad" syndrome.

ANANSI THE SPIDER

A TALE FROM THE ASHANTI

(1972)

INTRODUCING THE STORY

Anansi the Spider, Gerald McDermott's first picture book, had originally been created as an animated film. McDermott so effectively met the challenges of adapting a narrative with movement, spoken words, sound effects, and music onto the page that the book received a Caldecott Honor Medal as runner up to the most distinguished American picture book of the year. A work that appeared at a time when retellings of traditional African stories were gaining increased attention in the children's book field, it deals with the West African Ashanti hero.

Anansi the Spider introduced a large new audience to the work of Gerald McDermott. It contained themes and conflicts, as well as artistic techniques and designs, that he had explored in his films and that he would reexamine in new ways in his later books. The story is simple. When Anansi is first swallowed by a fish and later carried into the sky by a falcon, his six sons—each of whom has a special talent—must rescue him. Discovering a silver disk, the father decides to award it to the most deserving son. However, when they quarrel over who will receive the award, Nyame, The God of All Things, removes the disk to the sky.

Off he went, making a road.

They went fast, those six brothers, gone to help Anansi.

The story deals with the themes of wholeness and completeness, balance and harmony, mediation and moderation. Anansi, often the self-sufficient survivor, cannot help himself and is taken to both the depths and the heights, perhaps an (implicit) indication of the consequences of the kinds of character excesses and weaknesses he frequently exhibits in other stories. Only when the six brothers work cooperatively, when each is an integral part of a family unit, is Anansi restored to earth—the middle ground. However, the unity is broken because of the subsequent actions of each member of the family. Anansi becomes the failed father, breaking the bonds among the siblings by seeking to privilege one of them. The sons, through their quarrelling, complete the fragmentation of the family unit. Consequently, the reward they should have shared is lost to all.

The themes are presented in the form of two well-known Ashanti and, in general, African narrative genres. As a pourquoi tale, it explains the reasons for the moon's being in the sky. Ashanti people looking at the moon would be reminded of the story and, by extension, their culture's beliefs about the appropriate individual and family behavior that is implied in the characters and events. It is also a dilemma tale, after the telling of which, members of the audience would be invited to answer a question and to explain the reasons for their answers. In this case, the question would be: "Who do you think deserves the prize?" While there is no specific correct answer, the question invites respondents to consider the possibility that because the rescues had been collaborative efforts, the reward should probably have been shared—even if not equally.

The written text is short, containing only 365 words of spare, rhythmic prose. Much of the cultural and general meaning is communicated visually. In the illustrations, McDermott incorporated elements of Ashanti art and craftsmanship, particularly those relating to metalwork and weaving. The embossed pattern on the cover, which is not unlike those designs worked into metal, shows both a circle, symbolic of the moon and harmony, and, within it, fragments that represent both a spider web and the breakup of family unity. The endpapers introduce the patterns of weaving that also serve as backdrops for the illustrations within the story. Not only do the zig-zag lines parallel the literal fall, rise, and fall of Anansi, they also represent the thematic conflict of extremes. Embedded in the patterns are the symbols that represent the six sons. These McDermott based on the adinkra symbols that the Ashanti stamped on their cloth and that embodied a number of cultural concepts and values. The bold, almost electric primary and secondary colors used in the illustrations not only approximate those of Ashanti fabric dyes, they also communicate the tensions of the conflicts that permeate plot and themes.

THE AUTHOR DISCUSSES THE STORY

I think that when I started to transform the film into a picture book, the greatest challenge arose because I wasn't in control. That is, in a film, you establish the sequence and pace you want, and you move forward, using voice, music, and sound to lead the audience. There's a great deal of kinetic energy involved. None of this was available to me now. The readers determined the pace: they could go forward or backward, they could stop, they could flip pages at will. I needed to find ways of leading the readers through the book at a pace appropriate to the story. I also had to create on a flat page some of the energy found in the film.

I quickly discovered that my first assumption about the process wouldn't work. I couldn't just select twenty five or thirty of the four thousand stills from the film. I had to reimagine and recast the story. One of the important changes regarded color. I chose vivid colors to create a sense of vibration, of energy. The intensity of the hues had the effect of making the images appear to jump off the page. I remember one reviewer was shocked by the color and said something like, "I had to wear sunglasses."

Weaving became very important as a symbol for me. Not only were the Ashanti people who originated the story superb weavers, but their major story character, Anansi, was also a weaver. In some of their stories, he's a divine figure. He, like the creator, fashions a universe out of himself (out of his own matter). The weavers, like spiders, use threads to create an organic whole that's a work of art. In many ways, that's what I see the storyteller doing as well: weaving, like the spider, out of himself, out of his dreams, his subconscious, and, hopefully, like the Ashanti people, using colors and designs to make the finished product a work of art.

This was the first story in which I used symbols as identifying marks for the characters. Even though the silhouettes of each of the spiders are the same, the symbols reveal their individual talents and personalities. The idea came from looking at the adinkra cloth of the Ashanti. They carved the designs out of calabash gourds and stamped them on fabrics. I also used variations of some of the symbols as the background designs and in the trees and flowers. I used many symbols of the Ashanti world in depicting Nyame. As he was The God of All Things, it seemed appropriate that he should be represented by a wide range of symbols.

The book deals with a family theme, which has been an important aspect of many of my books. I wanted to use the web as a symbol of the interconnectedness of each member of the family. Each is part of a whole and each is linked, like the strands of the web. When they work together, they succeed; when they disagree, they lose the prize they should have had together. The role of the father is also interesting. Anansi doesn't provide leadership.

Engagement Activities

Before a **first reading**, the following activities may be interesting and useful, depending on the level of the students. In the early elementary grades, they may predict who might be the main character, based on the dust jacket cover, and, after noticing the spider's facial expression, can predict the tone of the story—from humorous to somber. If they have read any other Anansi stories, they can also suggest what his character traits might be and what kinds of actions might take place.

Students in middle and upper elementary grades can be introduced to the terms "Ashanti," "adinkra," and "Anansi" and then invited to find examples of Ashanti weaving. They can share the results of research on these topics and, when the story is introduced, can discuss how they can apply their background research to the story. (Note that the reading of other Anansi stories and the research into the cultural aspects can be used as extension activities.)

Look carefully at the embossed symbol on the hardcover edition and at the endpapers, noticing the details. After reading the story, students can reexamine these and discuss the relationships between the front matter and the story. Read the story, asking students to interrupt when they notice the beginning of a conflict; they should interrupt each time another problem is introduced. Record the students' observations. They should notice Anansi's being lost, falling into the ocean, being swallowed, then being carried into the sky and later falling. Read up to the point where the text states: "They were very happy that spider family." Ask the students if the story should be over at this point and, if so, why. Then explain that there are several pages to go and discuss why this might be so. There could be more conflicts. Continue the reading, noting the new conflicts.

Keep the final list for discussion later. Briefly discuss the appropriateness of the introductory material (cover, endpapers, etc.).

Before a **second reading**, have the students study the endpapers, looking for symbols and designs. Then quickly flip through the illustrations linking the symbols to specific spider sons. Reintroduce the list of conflicts and explain that the focus will be on linking the sons to the resolutions. To facilitate a discussion of the sons' roles, it might be useful beforehand to distribute a chart. The first column can depict the symbols; the second, the name of the son signified; the third, his actions in resolving or not resolving the conflicts; and, in the fourth, adjectives indicating his character and personality. (The fourth column can be completed after a discussion of all the conflicts and resolutions.) In discussing the conflicts, students can consider why the sons' actions at first lead to positive resolutions and why, in the later part of the story, the actions of both father and sons lead to a negative resolution.

Before a **third reading**, students who are familiar with other Anansi stories can discuss elements of Anansi's character, such as cleverness and foolishness, selfishness and selflessness, and can notice that he sometimes succeeds and sometimes fails. Students unfamiliar with these stories can be presented with these facts. When they listen to a rereading of the story, they can examine Anansi's facial expressions and body language to see how in this story he is similar to and different from other ones and the extent to which he is responsible for his predicaments.

Having considered the various characters, conflicts, and themes, readers can then discuss how the visuals communicate these. For example, the cover symbol can represent the moon and spider web, unity and fragmentation; the zig-zag of the weaving pattern reflects the literal and symbolic fates of Anansi. The web can be seen as symbol of unity; however, during the quarrel it becomes smaller and the spiders lose their distinctness. The designs that make up Nyame can be linked to designs found elsewhere in the book. Students can discuss how using these to make up the God's figure is appropriate for one who is "The God of All Things."

Students can enter the words that describe the emotions and characters of Anansi, the sons, and Nyame into their "Dictionary of Character and Emotions."

Extension Activities

Literature: The story invites comparison with other McDermott stories involving falls from the sky. In what way are the causes and end results of Anansi's story similar to or different from those of Icarus (*Sunflight*), Coyote, Daniel O'Rourke, and Jabutí? Discussion should deal not only with external circumstances but also with the characters and motivations of those individuals who fall and those (if they are different individuals) who cause the falls. Like *Papagayo*, this is a pourquoi story about the moon. *Papagayo* explains the waning and waxing of the moon; *Anansi the Spider*, the reason the moon is in the sky. The causes for these characteristics of the moon are not "scientific," but they relate to the behaviors and personalities of characters. Students might wish to discuss the "character causes" in these stories. Interestingly, although McDermott tells stories about two characters separated by the Atlantic Ocean, both stories relate to the consequences of individuals cooperating or failing to do so. Have the students notice that McDermott is more interested in the human psychology the characters and their actions reveal than in explanations about elements of the natural world.

In Gail Haley's *A Story, a Story*, Ananse (another spelling of the name) interacts with the sky god and uses his own wits to benefit others, while in Tololwa Mollel's *Ananse's Feast*, the trickster's selfish conniving backfires. Students in the upper elementary grades may wish to read these stories, along with those found in Peggy Appiah's *Tales of an Ashanti Father*, as the starting point for a discussion of the complex and often contradictory nature of the character. By comparing these stories with the ones found in Philip Sherlock's *West Indian Folk-tales*, students can see how the character was slightly modified in narratives that were carried by slaves to the Caribbean.

Elphinstone Dayrell's *Why the Sun and Moon Live in the Sky* is another African pourquoi story about the moon's celestial location. John Steptoe's *Mufaro's Beautiful Daughters* also deals with the relationships between siblings, while Margaret Mahy's *The Seven Chinese Brothers* discusses the results of the cooperative actions of brothers.

Language Arts: McDermott's very spare text includes almost no dialogue and thus provides many opportunities for readers at all levels to provide dialogue and additional description and narrative. After looking at Anansi's facial expressions at specific points in the story and discussing the events, students can create dialogue balloons for what Anansi is saying and thinking. Older students who have studied several Anansi stories and who have become aware of the different facets of his personality might work at having the Spider's thoughts and words reveal character traits. The scenes in which the sons quarrel also present interesting dialogue possibilities!

African dilemma stories frequently concluded with the storyteller asking a question to the audience. There were neither correct nor incorrect answers, only convincing, well-argued as opposed to unconvincing, poorly argued ones. Implicit in *Anansi the Spider* are the questions, "To whom would you award the silver disk and why?" General class discussions should be encouraged, and sometimes responses should be challenged by the discussion leader or other students to make sure arguments offered are as convincing as possible. In this way, participants are not only replicating a traditional West African storytelling experience, they are also sharpening their own skills in developing strong, logical arguments. Students in the upper grades can also write clear, concise one-paragraph briefs supporting their claim that a certain son deserves the prize.

Social Studies: In addition to discussing how the story reflects some of the values of the Ashanti people, students can also consider how aspects of that West African culture influenced McDermott's presentation and interpretation of it. By using weaving patterns and adinkra-like symbols, how did he communicate the deeper cultural implications? Students who briefly researched these elements before reading the story (see Engagement Activities) can extend their research. The arts of most traditional cultures were not merely decorative; they reflected and embodied social and spiritual beliefs. Creating a work of art placed a great deal of responsibility on the artist.

The adinkra symbols are discussed on a free website: www.welltempered . net/adinkra/. These symbols were often stamped onto woven cloth so that, to use a title given to one website on the topic, the cloth truly was a "social fabric." Students can study the meanings of the symbols found on the website and can suggest which of these could represent character traits, emotions, themes, and conflicts of the story.

Fine Arts, Film, Drama: Students who have learned about adinkra cloth and symbols applicable to the story might wish to create their own adinkra cloth about the story, choosing appropriate colors, patterns, and symbols. This activity could also be applied to other Ashanti stories they may have read.

After noting that *Anansi the Spider* was the first book that McDermott adapted from one of his films, ask students to discuss how the story might have been presented as a film and what challenges the author might have faced in retelling the story as a book. Show the movie, after which viewers can add to their list of film techniques used. Then reread the book, asking students to notice particularly the means used to adapt the story. Students can then consider these questions. Which of the two presentations do they consider most effective and why? Do they think that there are any differences of meaning between the two?

Professor Christine Doyle of Central Connecticut University has had elementary students act out *Anansi the Spider* and has offered these suggestions. "The simple structure of the folktale, as well as the large number of characters (ten, including the narrator), make it ideal for classroom dramatizations in the early elementary grades. The character symbols can be rendered on construction paper and affixed to shirts to identify Anansi and his sons. A crown or cape could identify the Sky God. Additional readily available props include several sheets of construction paper for Road Builder to lay down, a blue sheet or blanket to represent the river that could be thrown over Anansi and Fish and that River Drinker could gather up as he 'drinks up' the river, a Nerf Ball for Stone Thrower to hurl at Falcon, and a pillow or cushion for catching Anansi. A white helium-filled balllon to serve as the moon could provide a dramatic effect when Nyame releases it into the sky at the end. Probably two or three performances of the story could include every child in most classrooms."

References

Appiah, Peggy, reteller. *Tales of an Ashanti Father*. London: Andre Deutsch, 1967.

Dayrell, Elphinstone, reteller. Illustrated by Blair Lent. *Why the Sun and the Moon Live in the Sky*. Boston: Houghton Mifflin, 1968.

Haley, Gail E., reteller and illustrator. *A Story, a Story*. New York: Atheneum, 1970.

Mahy, Margaret, reteller. Illustrated by Jean and Mou-sien Tseng. *The Seven Chinese Brothers*. New York: Scholastic, 1990.

Mollel, Tololwa M., reteller. Illustrated by Andrew Glass. *Ananse's Feast: An Ashanti Tale*. New York: Clarion Books, 1997.

Philip Sherlock, reteller. Illustrated by Joan Kiddell-Monroe. *West Indian Folk-tales*. Oxford: Oxford University Press, 1966.

Steptoe, John, reteller. *Mufaro's Beautiful Daughters: An African Tale*. New York: Lothrop, Lee, & Shepard, 1987.

ARROW TO THE SUN
A PUEBLO INDIAN TALE

(1974)

INTRODUCING THE STORY

Arrow to the Sun deals with a familiar children's literature theme: an outcast child proves his special qualities and becomes a hero within his society. Son of the Lord of the Sun and a Pueblo maiden, the Boy, ridiculed by his peers, embarks on a long, difficult journey to find his father, passes a series of dangerous tests, and returns to his village bringing the gift of life to the people. However, it is more than a variation of a staple plot in children's stories. It also includes McDermott's interest in "the individual on a quest to achieve self-fulfillment," major features of traditional Pueblo culture, and concepts explained by Joseph Campbell about the characteristics of heroes from around the world. These elements are communicated through both words and pictures.

On one level, color, design, and details communicate the changing status of the Boy from social outcast to celebrated leader. The gradual introduction of a full spectrum of color from the middle of the story onward indicates the growth of the Boy's sense of fulfillment and, therefore, happiness. Details in the depiction of him also indicate the changes. Rejected by his peers, he appears small on

The people celebrated his return in the Dance of Life.

a two-page spread and is located on the side, with a frown on his face. In the final illustration, as he leads the people in the Dance of Life, he is located front and center, the dominant figure on the page, a smile on his face.

On a deeper level, the visuals invest the story with implicit meanings linked to the cultural and religious beliefs of the traditional Pueblo people of the American Southwest. Agrarians, whose main harvest was corn, they believed that a successful crop depended not only on rain and appropriate horticultural practices but also on the achievement of a good relationship with the spiritual powers who controlled all aspects of life on earth. At the beginning of the story, the Boy, whose logo is a stylized cross-section of an ear of corn, lives in an arid land symbolized by the dominant orange color. To this place, he brings the rainbow, the gift of his father, and the symbol of sun and rain. The manner in which he proves himself is deeply rooted in the people's beliefs. The mountain lions, symbolizing war, are tamed; the Boy has established the peace necessary for

agriculture. Rattlesnakes, used in rainmaking ceremonies, are formed into a circle; the Boy has accorded them spiritual respect. By forcing the bees to order themselves into a functioning hive, he establishes the organization and cooperation necessary for the process of pollenization. Finally, by submitting to the spiritual energy of his father, symbolized by the lightning, he is able to bring the Lord's powers to the earth.

The visual elements reveal the influences of Joseph Campbell's ideas in *The Hero with a Thousand Faces*. Early in his life Campbell writes, "The typical hero finds himself [in a world that] suffers from a symbolic deficiency" (Campbell 37). The dominant oranges early in the book reflect this deficiency. The arid land parallels the spiritual state of the people who jeer at and reject the Boy. His search for his father fits well with the quest as described by Campbell: "The child of destiny has to face a long period of obscurity. . . . He is thrown inward to his own depths or outward to the unknown. . . . Alone in some little room the young world apprentice learns the lesson of the seed powers" (Campbell 326–27). For the Boy, this involves traveling through the dark heavens and entering the four kiva chambers. After having been transformed, he brings the full rainbow, the gift of Life, to his people. Campbell writes, "The effect of the successful adventure of the hero is the unlocking and release of the flow of life into the body of the world" (Campbell 40). At the end of the story, the Boy dances on the rainbow. The circular designs and abundant colors indicate the unity and spiritual vitality he has given to people who once rejected him.

THE AUTHOR DISCUSSES THE STORY

I think that *Arrow to the Sun*, like so many of my stories—especially the earlier ones—is about the task of self-creation. The whole point of these stories is for the individual to go on a quest, experience a test, overcome the obstacles, be transformed, then return filled with the wisdom and power to serve others. The adventures of the central figure embody the guiding principles for the societies or cultures who told the stories. The main difference between this story and my earlier ones is that here the quester does not fail.

I've always admired and been fascinated by the art of Pueblo cultures, and my graphic style really grew out of a combination of the influence of folk art style, the simple bold approach to symbolism and color—as is the case for the Pueblo people—as well as my training in contemporary graphics. It was Joseph Campbell who suggested that I look at the art of the Native cultures of the Southwest. I became fascinated by such elements as the step design, and the weaving and sand painting of the Navajo people, and I started to delve into the tales of the area. That's how I discovered, or was discovered by, the quest tale of a boy in search of his father. I originally turned to film to express these ideas and then, almost simultaneously, began to develop the story in book form as well.

I hadn't been to the Southwest when I decided to work on the book. But I engaged in extensive research. I immersed myself in Pueblo culture, not to be able to copy it, but to acquire a sense of the organic logic of design and structure so that I could distill it through my own sensibilities. Two elements of the culture particularly embodied key aspects of the story: corn and the sun. The sun is a universal symbol; the psychologist Carl Jung related it to the individual's sense of fulfillment and identity. For the agrarian Pueblo people, it was central to their lives and the focus of many of their spiritual rituals. Corn, of course, was the main crop, and it depended on the sun. I was looking for a symbol for these elements and I noticed the design of a cross-section of an ear of corn. It became the Boy's logo, a representation of his power to link the worlds of earth and sky.

When I first visited the Pueblos of New Mexico long after *Arrow to the Sun* had been published, I found out that many communities had been using the book for years to introduce children to aspects of their traditional culture. I was honored and gratified.

Engagement Activities

No matter what the age or grade level of children to whom this story is being presented, it is best introduced as picture book. Depending on the audience, cultural and cross-cultural aspects can be considered at greater or less depth.

Before a **first reading**, briefly present the setting of the story, the southwestern desert area of the United States, and note that the traditional Pueblo people grew corn as their major vegetable food. Explain that, in the summer, there is a great deal of sun, frequent thunderstorms, and some, but not much rain. Have the students notice the details and colors on the cover, endpapers, and title, copyright, and dedication pages. The importance of these can be discussed at various times during follow-up discussions. Do draw the students' attention to the sun-corn symbol on the (original) cover and the dedication page and ask them to look for it in following illustrations.

Read the story through, giving viewers plenty of time to look at the pictures. For each of the wordless illustrations of the Boy's entrance into and departure from the four kivas, briefly ask the children what changes he has effected. You may wish to explain that lions are mountain lions or cougars and that the serpents are rattlesnakes. After reading, briefly return to the cover or dedication page and ask the students where the logo is seen in the story.

Before a **second reading**, lead a general discussion of children's responses to the story. After rereading the story, have them discuss the Boy's status before he begins his journey and after he returns to his village. To do this, it is useful to have two copies of the book, so that the pictures of his being mocked and driven away by the others and his leading the Dance of Life can be displayed side by side. Start with a comparison of details in the two pictures, noticing such aspects as change in colors and the difference of the size, appearance, and location of the Boy. Children can then be invited to provide a list of words for his emotions in the earlier and later pictures and to suggest reasons for the changes in his emotions. They can then return to the pictures looking for visual evidence to support their interpretations of the Boy's emotions. Students can enter appropriate words into their "Dictionary of Character and Emotions."

At this point, students can be introduced (or reintroduced) to the concept of conflict: the introduction of problems or difficulties for a character. Major conflicts are usually introduced at the beginning of a story and not resolved until the conclusion. Ask students to identify the main conflict in this story and how the Boy goes about resolving it. Does he face any intermediate conflicts in his journey? How do his responses to these help him to resolve the major conflict? Discuss the final resolution and what it reveals about the Boy's character.

Have the students notice the change from the "dry" orange colors that dominate the earlier pages to a fuller spectrum in the later ones. Have them point out when the change begins to occur—when he is shot through the heavens to the Sun, the home of his father. Does the color change indicate a change in emotions, and if there is an emotional change, is it related in any way to the Boy's successfully having resolved intermediate conflicts and to his moving closer to a resolution of the main conflict? Explain that McDermott is using color change to indicate both shifting emotions and a movement toward conflict resolution.

Before a **third reading** of the story, cut two or three ears of corn into circular pieces. (Note that it might be a good idea to let the cut pieces dry out a few days.) Pass the circles to the students, asking them to look at the circle to see if it reminds them of anything. Before the activity, do not mention the book, thus giving them a chance to make the connection with the Boy's symbol on their own. Ask them what the symbol stands for—corn. Then suggest that it may also stand for something else in the story—the sun. Remind them of the earlier discussion of the southwestern landscape and the agrarian basis of Pueblo culture, and then ask why the symbol might be a good one for the Boy. This discussion can lead into a consideration of the story in culture-specific terms.

In the lower grades, this examination of the story can begin by asking the students what is needed for the growth of corn—sun and rain. However, when we look at the colors of the early pictures we can see that the rains have not come. The dominant oranges suggest aridity. After the Boy has passed the kiva tests, what is streaming behind him—a rainbow. Students should then discuss what two elements (sun and rain) are necessary to produce a rainbow. They should note that the Boy shares the rainbow with the people who had once been unkind to him. Why is it important that he shares the rainbow? It is because he is giving them the sun and rain they need for their crops to grow. The dancers, they should note, celebrate the tests he passed and the growing corn.

In the higher grades, this discussion can be supplemented with an examination of the specific Pueblo significance of each of the kivas, what the Boy does in each, and why his actions there are important. He bravely tames, but does not kill, lions, symbols of war; he respectfully creates a symbol of harmony and unity from the rattlesnakes, which were part of the rain dance ceremonies; he develops a spirit of cooperation needed for successful farming by organizing the bees. Before discussing the fourth kiva, ask the students if they can see any significance in the sequence of the earlier kivas. Is it important that each of the animals is smaller? Is it, perhaps, more difficult to organize the bees than to tame the lions?

Then explain that, unlike European stories, where tests are usually in threes, in many Native cultures, four is a number representing completeness. Then mention that not only is lightning part of a thunderstorm that could bring rain, but also that it is, in many Native cultures, the sign of the presence of spirit power, in this case the power of the Lord of the Sun. What happens to the Boy in the fourth kiva? He receives his father's power. The rainbow he brings home is a gift he has received because he has proved to his father that he is worthy.

Discuss with the students characteristics of a hero, noting their responses on the board. Ask them then to consider events of this story and to see which of their suggestions apply. Ask them to add any other aspects that they think make the boy a hero. Finally, ask them to discuss how, specifically, the Boy could be considered a hero in traditional Pueblo culture? How could he be considered heroic to modern non-Pueblo readers?

Extension Activities

Literature: Students in the middle and upper elementary grades who are studying several of McDermott's works can compare the Boy's visit to the sun with those of Wind (in *Musicians of the Sun*) and Raven. After noticing similarities in the journeys, particularly the fact that they result in a betterment of life for people on earth, students can discuss differences in the heroes, such as their original status, the reasons for their quests, and their actions in achieving their goals. Students can also note how each of these stories, in addition to the similarities, reflects the cultural values of specific cultures.

Students in the early elementary grades can compare and contrast the Boy to other unlikely heroes such as those found in Leo Lionni's *Frederick*, Jeanne M. Lee's *Toad Is the Uncle of Heaven*, and Taro Yashima's *Crow Boy*. In the upper elementary grades, the Boy's quest journey and relationship with his society can be compared to those of the heroes in the English legend *The Kitchen Knight* (Margaret Hodges), the Japanese hero tale *Momotaro: The Peach Boy* (Linda Shute), and Blackfoot myth *The Legend of Scarface* (Robert San Souci). The last work, from the Blackfoot, a hunting people of the northwestern plains, involves the sun journey of a rejected youth and provides an interesting series of parallels with McDermott's story from a southwestern agricultural community. In studying heroes from a variety of cultures, students can notice both shared traits and culturally unique characteristics.

Language Arts: *Arrow to the sun* represents McDermott's "non-use" of words at its best and, as such, reflects his belief in the importance of reader and viewer involvement in the creation of a story's meaning. In order to "make meaning," readers must carefully notice the details of those illustrations unaccompanied by written text. They can examine the double-spread of the Boy's trip to the sun, the three paired illustrations of his *entering* and *exiting* kivas, and the single illustration of him *in* the final kiva. The double-spread implies a series of events as the arrow moves through time and space, the paired illustrations imply actions that occur between the pictures, and the single illustration implies a number of complex emotional and physical responses on the part of the Boy. Students can create written texts that include descriptions of settings, accounts of actions and events, and records of the Boy's emotions and thoughts.

Social Studies: Although the Dance of Life depicted on the final page of the story is McDermott's own creation, it is true in spirit to the agrarian culture he depicts in the story. The Pueblo people marked stages in the cycle of the planting, growth, and harvest of the corn with ceremonies that honored the spirit beings who were responsible for the success of the crop. These events demonstrated the people's respect toward and reverence for their natural and spiritual environments. During the ceremonies, kachina dancers, with figures representing the various spirit powers, performed. Students may wish to research the various traditional ceremonies, noticing when they were performed and how and why they embodied the spiritual elements essential for the growth of a good crop. It is **extremely important**, however, that students realize that these were and still are sacred ceremonies and that photographing or drawing dancers is permitted only with specific permission from the various Pueblos. **Therefore, teachers should not encourage the drawing or photocopying of representations of these sacred ceremonies**.

One interesting aspect of Pueblo culture that can be shared with students involves a method of traditional religious and spiritual instruction. Children were frequently presented with carved figures representing the various spiritual beings (kachinas). These kachina dolls, as they are called, are not in themselves sacred, but they were intended to provide children with visual aids for remembering spiritual powers. These figures are now widely available in Native American gift stores and, depending on their size and the quality of craftsmanship, range in price from ten or twenty dollars to hundreds or, occasionally, thousands of dollars. A few of the smaller, less expensive figures could be displayed both to introduce students to elements of Pueblo art and religious instruction and to help them understand one of the sources that McDermott drew on in creating his own illustrations.

The Arts: Because McDermott conceived *Arrow to the sun* as both a book and a film rather than as a book adaptation of one of his earlier films, the story provides students with an excellent opportunity to examine not only two versions of the same narrative but also the unique resources of each medium for storytelling. Before students view the film, they should refamiliarize themselves with details of the book and be invited to keep notes, as they watch, of differences between the two versions of the same tale. After a viewing, they can discuss generally the differences between presenting a story in the two mediums, noting particularly the fact that films can present movement, including a continuous sequence of events, and can use sound—dialogue, music, and background sounds—to communicate meaning. In *Arrow to the sun*, specifically, the sound and movement allow McDermott to present the entire story as a stylized dance and, in the case of the Boy's tests, to depict what happens in each kiva. Students can also notice and discuss possible reasons for the inclusion of a lizard, a turkey, and a butterfly during the earlier part of the Boy's search. Finally, they can offer explanations for the addition of the corn maiden after the Boy's return to earth and her role in the concluding dance.

If students have written narratives about the Boy's experiences in the kivas, they can compare their versions with those of the film, and, using graph paper, can illustrate their own accounts.

References

Campbell, Joseph. *The Hero with a Thousand Faces*. Princeton, NJ: Princeton University Press, 1949.

Hodges, Margaret, reteller. Illustrated by Trina Schart Hyman. *The Kitchen Knight: A Tale of King Arthur*. New York: Holiday House, 1990.

Lee, Jeanne M., reteller and illustrator. *Toad Is the Uncle of Heaven: A Vietnamese Folktale*. New York: Holt, Rinehart, and Winston, 1985.

Lionni, Leo. *Frederick*. New York: Pantheon, 1967.

San Souci, Robert, reteller. Illustrated by Daniel San Souci. *The Legend of Scarface: A Black-foot Indian Tale.* Garden City, NY: Doubleday and Company, 1978.

Shute, Linda, reteller and illustrator. *Momotaro, the Peach Boy: A Traditional Japanese Tale.* New York: Lothrop, Lee, and Shepard, 1986.

Yashima, Taro. *Crow Boy.* New York: Viking Press, 1955.

THE STONECUTTER

A JAPANESE FOLKTALE

(1975)

INTRODUCING THE STORY

One of four of his early animated films that he redeveloped as picture books, *The Stonecutter* is based on a traditional Japanese tale McDermott had enjoyed reading as a child. Interestingly, early versions of this story in English are about a greedy person who comes to understand and repent of his mistakes and to live contented with his lot in life. McDermott's story is, as were

many of his films, a narrative about an individual who fails in a quest because of personal limitations.

Tasaku, the central character—whose name echoes the Japanese word *dasaku*, meaning "work of poor, inferior quality"—begins his story as a humble but happy laborer whose work provides the materials out of which palaces and temples are built. However, he suddenly becomes envious of the wealth and fame of a passing prince. The spirit who lives in the mountain, because he admires the man's simple contentment, grants Tasaku's wish to be a prince. However, the transformation and its attendant power do not bring well-being to the stonecutter, and he successively seeks to be changed into the sun, a cloud, and a mountain—all of which he perceives to be more powerful. However, he does not use power beneficently, causing drought, storm, and destruction. His final desire, which, the text notes, is *demanded* rather than *wished, wanted,* or *told,* as were the others, proves his undoing. As a mountain, he is powerless against the actions of another "lowly stonecutter, chipping away at his feet."

It is interesting to note that, like many McDermott stories, *The Stonecutter* involves the sun, but that, whereas other characters wish to use the sun to help others, Tasaku becomes the sun and employs its strength to gratify his increasingly selfish need for power. It is an appropriately ironic conclusion to the story that he finally becomes powerless, not all-powerful, at the mercy of a human being as unimportant as he once was. He has not become the integrated individual, aware of who he is and where he belongs, something that the Boy in *Arrow to the Sun*, who brings the sun's generative powers of warmth and rain to his people, does. His transformations are not earned; they are accomplished by the spirit, an outside source. It is his failure to perform actions worthy of his new incarnations that dooms him, renders him finally incapable of any action. For attempting to violate his nature and, implicitly, for violating the hierarchical organization of traditional Japanese society, the stonecutter is no longer able to participate in the activity that, as an expression of his innate character, brought him fulfillment. He now trembles in fear.

McDermott's art, in its use of Japanese styles of wood-block print and banner making, combined with his own sense of graphic design, embodies the traditional elements of the tale. His use of both color and design also reinforces his interpretation of the ancient story. The illustrations are created from shapes cut from hand-painted white paper colored with poster paints. The brush strokes, along with the vertical shape of the book, suggest the theme of the central character's rise and fall.

Each of the illustrations, with two exceptions (those with emperors and their subjects), makes limited use of color. In the opening and closing scenes, in which the position of the mountain and the person cutting stone are reversed, as is Tasaku's situation, green dominates, indicating a sense of harmony and balance, a sense reinforced by the gentle flow of line patterns. However, as the central character seeks greater power, harsh oranges, reds, and browns become more dominant. Appropriately, in the two wordless double-spreads, where Tasaku unleashes destruction, green is completely absent. Dark blues and grays parallel the darkening of Tasaku's character and, perhaps, the increasing unhappiness of the spirit. As the conflict moves to its ironic resolution, green again returns to the illustrations.

The Japanese custom of bowing to show respect is used in the illustrations to reveal Tasaku's changing opinion of his new selves and his attitude to the world around. At the beginning, he is on his knees, working contentedly, accepting of his lowly status. However, he is standing, rather than bowing, before the passing emperor, to whom he should show respect. Only once more does he kneel, when the sun devastates his garden. But in his pride, he quickly stands and then ascends to become the sun. Immediately after, people bow before him in supplication and fear.

Tasaku's transformations are also indicated by the designs—introduced on the title page—associated with him. These have been inspired by Japanese use of abstract symbols. The rectangular form symbolic of his natural, stonecutter state is replaced by a four-piece diamond form, and then a six-armed figure. This is a variation of the two-tied sash of his working kimono and the three-tailed one he wears as an emperor. His power is increasing. The cloud symbol is appropriately a somber-hued gray and black. The mountain symbol is once again green; but Tasaku is not acting, he is acted upon. The new stonecutter has block symbols, but these have diamond shapes in them. Is he, too, going to follow Tasaku's unfortunate path?

THE AUTHOR DISCUSSES THE STORY

When I was a young boy, the story of the stonecutter was one of my favorites. I think that I was fascinated by the idea of folktale and legend even at that age, and so it's not surprising that when I set about to make my first film around 1960, I chose that story. In 1975, I recast the tale as a picture book. Looking back, I see that in the first traditional story I retold, I chose a theme that would become central to my work: the quest for self-transformation, for self-fulfillment. Tasaku has not grown into the roles he chooses. The power that he acquires can be used to control others or to energize them; he has a choice between manipulation and creation. Using power to alter others or to force them to his way dooms the one who exercises the power. Tasaku fails as a leader and an individual.

Creating the picture book was in no way a matter of taking a select number of important "stills" from the film. I engaged in extensive research into traditional Japanese art so that I could relate the story in a way that combined the cultural values and my own response. I chose collage as the medium for the illustrations and a vertical, rather than horizontal, shape for the book. The collage, with its sharp edges and liquid watercolor textures, gave the effect of traditional Japanese art; the vertical shape was appropriate for Tasaku's journey. For the book, I also designed symbols to represent the character's transformations. In addition, I depicted the figure of the spirit, who, except for his hands, wasn't seen in the film. Just before I submitted the final art work to the publishers, I decided to revise the final picture and showed Tasaku's shape in the mountain. These changes represented his final state—the end of his quest for selfish power.

Engagement Activities

Before a **first reading**, have the students look carefully at the dust jacket cover, cover, endpapers, title page, copyright page, and back dust jacket cover. Have them make a list of items or details that they think could be significant in the story. Possible items include the building, the colors red and black, the symbols, and the banner stripes. Keep the list on the board and pause occasionally during the reading to give students a chance to glance at it. After the story is finished, students can offer their explanations about the significance of the items.

Ask the students to look for conflicts and their resolutions during the reading. Read the first three pages, giving time for studying the illustrations. Ask if there is any conflict yet. The children should note that at this point Tasaku is content. After reading the story, have them discuss the cause of Tasaku's initial conflict, focusing on his envy. Is he satisfied when his initial conflict is resolved? Have them notice that the conflict is resolved by the spirit. Discuss how

Tasaku's attitudes to the resolutions for each sequential conflict reveal his character. How is the conflict finally resolved? Discuss why the spirit leaves him after granting his final request. Why and how is Tasaku responsible for his final situation?

During a **second reading**, have the students carefully observe the illustrations to see how these communicate the various stages of the conflict. Begin by having them compare the first and last double-spreads of the stonecutter and the mountain, noticing all the differences, including the reversal of the images, the position of Tasaku, and the differences between him and the new stonecutter and between the piles of cut stone. How do the contrasts reflect Tasaku's altered circumstances? Both illustrations are dominated by the color green, which suggests contentment, and both have black lines in the mountain. But whereas the first picture embodies Tasaku's sense of well-being, the last does not. As you reread, have the students notice the dominant color for each of the pictures and discuss how this color reflects the nature of the conflict at that point.

Before a **third reading**, briefly discuss the symbols found on the title page and have the students notice when they appear in the story. Explain that they represent the various transformations of Tasaku. Before the reading, the students can be given copies of a chart on which they record Tasaku's transformations. In the first column they can draw a picture of each logo and what stage of Tasaku's "development" it reflects (stonecutter, emperor, etc.). In the second column, they can list what he does in each role. In the third, they can note what he could have done with his new power. In the fourth, they can note the exact words he uses to the spirit when he wants to be changed. They can complete one line for each of the transformations as they listen to the reading. They might notice that in the last transformation, he isn't able to do anything or to ask anything. He is powerless and the spirit has left him. Students can then use the completed chart as the basis for a discussion of Tasaku's character. They can discuss whether McDermott's ironic ending is appropriate, or whether the stonecutter should be returned to his original form and be content, as he was in earlier versions of the story. After the discussion, the students can work on their "Dictionary of Character and Emotions."

Extension Activities

Literature: Many of McDermott's earlier works delineate failed quests. Students can examine the fates of Mavungu (*The Magic Tree*), Icarus (*Sunflight*), and the spider's sons (*Anansi the spider*). As with Tasaku, character weaknesses result in the main figures being unable to achieve fulfillment. After having examined the stonecutter's flaws, the students can compare these with the weaknesses of the other failed characters.

The story invites comparison with other Japanese traditional stories. In *Momotaro* (Linda Shute), the hero also goes on a circular journey, but because he works with companions and makes his quest for the benefit of others, he returns home successful. In *The Crane Wife* (Sumika Yagawa), a poor man loses a devoted wife and lives a lonely, grief-stricken life because of his greed and self-centeredness.

Many traditional tales around the world deal with the theme "Be careful what you wish for, you might get it." The Grimm Brothers' *The Fisherman and His Wife* (Margo Zemach) also recounts an ironic circular journey and a magical, wish-granting being. Because this story focuses on two people—a husband and wife—it also explores the nature of the relationship between the two. *Hey, Al* (Arthur Yorinks), a modern picture book, humorously traces the fortunes of a man and his dog when they find themselves in an apparently perfect environment. They, too, make a circular journey, but return home contented with their original dwelling. Phoebe Gilman's *The Gypsy Princess* also portrays a person who, when she gets what she wishes for, becomes very unhappy and is glad when she returns to her humble life.

Language Arts: McDermott includes two wordless double-spreads in the book, both of them depicting Tasaku's destructive actions. After carefully studying the color, design, and details of each of the pictures and discussing what these communicate, students can write a paragraph in which they provide action and description. More confident writers may wish to write their paragraphs from the point-of-view of Tasaku or one of the victims of the destruction, giving the speaker's reactions to events.

The spirit appears in six illustrations, listening to or acting on Tasaku's desires. However, even though the narrative suggests some of the spirit's reactions, he is given no dialogue. Students, perhaps working in groups, can create the spirit's thoughts and words, many of which could be judgmental comments on the stonecutter's actions and attitudes.

Social Studies: Respect for others and recognition and acceptance of one's social status were important elements of traditional Japanese culture. One method of acknowledging one's humbleness and demonstrating respect for those higher was to bow. Have students notice when Tasaku bows and when, often inappropriately, he does not. For example, he is on his knees at the beginning, contentedly working, but stands before the emperor. Students should discuss how traditional readers of the story would judge Tasaku's changing reactions to himself and others. They can then explain what cultural values the story would have had for traditional Japanese people.

The Arts: Fifteen years separate the creation of the film and book adaptations of *The Stonecutter*. In fact, in returning to the book, McDermott essentially recreated the art and, implicitly, subtly reinterpreted the traditional story. Students in the upper elementary grades will enjoy noting the differences between the 1960 animated film and the 1975 picture book. Before screening the film, reread the book with the students so that visual and verbal details are fresh in their minds. Show the film, inviting the viewers to note differences; look again at the book, and then have the students view the film a second time, updating their lists of differences. In addition to noting small alterations in the language, students may wish to consider the book's extensive use of the color green, the depiction of Tasaku in the mountain, and the addition of the mountain spirit. Having noted the differences, they can discuss how the changes influenced the meaning of the story in its book form.

Students may be interested in studying both traditional Japanese banner art and McDermott's collage technique (which is described on the book's copyright page). Then they might create banners that would be appropriate to heroes from other traditional Japanese stories. They could also create collage illustrations for other folktales, deciding what colors would be most appropriate for the papers they will be cutting out for their own illustrations.

References

Gilman, Phoebe. *The Gypsy Princess.* Toronto: North Winds Press, 1995.

Jarrell, Randal, translator. Illustrated by Margo Zemach. *The Fisherman and His Wife: A Tale from the Brothers Grimm.* New York: Farrar, Straus, Giroux, 1980.

Shute, Linda, reteller and illustrator. *Momotaro: The Peach Boy: A Traditional Japanese Story.* New York: Lothrop, Lee & Shepard, 1986.

Yagawa, Sumiko, reteller. Translated by Katherine Paterson. Illustrated by Suekichi Akaba. *The Crane Wife.* New York: William Morrow and Company, 1981.

Yorinks, Arthur. Illustrated by Richard Egielski. *Hey, Al.* New York: Farrar, Straus, Giroux, 1986.

PAPAGAYO THE MISCHIEF MAKER

(1980)

INTRODUCING THE STORY

An original story by Gerald McDermott, *Papagayo* uses as its central character the trickster bird found in Brazilian folktales. It recounts how the raucous parrot delighted in pestering the night creatures as they tried to sleep during the day. But when the ghost of an ancient monster dog appeared in the sky, eating away the moon, Papagayo came to the rescue, using his noise-making abilities and

encouraging the terrified night creatures to develop theirs. Frightened by the racket, the moon-eater fled, and the animals congratulated themselves on their cleverness and courage. While they no longer complained about the parrot's daytime noise making, they ignored his warnings that the monster would certainly return.

That night, Papagayo kept a vigil with the night creatures. It was very dark, because the moon was now just a slender crescent, but Papagayo tried hard to stay awake. He was just about to doze off when he heard the creatures whimpering.

The moon-dog had returned and he was bigger and fatter than ever. He greedily licked the last sweet bit of the moon.

The story presents many sharp conflicts and contrasts: the individual and the group, cleverness and cowardice, selfishness and cooperation, supernatural and natural creatures, day and night, above and below ground, noise and quietness, activity and inertia. When Papagayo is able to control his energetic behavior, channeling it to constructive uses, and the night creatures take his advice and overcome their timidity and inertia, the major conflict—the impending loss of the moon, whose subdued light the creatures need—is resolved. However, this resolution is unstable. Papagayo goes back to his daytime noise making, and the animals do not pay attention to his advice at the end.

The story is written in the form of a pourquoi legend—an explanation of the origin of natural characteristics, in this case, the monthly waning of the moon. However, it is much more than a discussion of a natural phenomenon, as McDermott also adds subtle analysis of the character of the hero and of the group psychology of the night creatures, making the story about general human emotions and conflicts.

THE AUTHOR DISCUSSES THE STORY

I'd been reading folktales from Brazil and had become very interested in the personality of Papagayo, the traditional trickster. But none of the stories about him seemed to be suitable for children. They were too complex or too "adult" in their content. But I was really fascinated by the parrot: he was so colorful, both literally and in terms of his personality. He was raucous, filled with energy and vitality, and he was also full of himself. I decided to create my own story so that I could embody in words and pictures the qualities of his personality. One of the things I wanted to capture in my story was the contrast between Papagayo and the night creatures: his "over-the-top enthusiasm" and their timidity.

At that time, I was also very interested in the nature of the unconscious elements of our being and their relationship to our conscious lives. The ghost of the monster dog, long dormant underground and then leaping into activity above the ground, into the sky, symbolizes this. When it arrives, it's voracious and all consuming—this is very dangerous. When all the creatures act together to drive the dog back into its proper place, you have a symbol of the healthy, integrated personality. But the dog will be back; the struggle to maintain balance is an ongoing conflict.

When I set about creating the visual elements of the story, I wanted to emphasize the thematic contrasts. The white of the day and the deep blue of the night reflected the two time periods, the worlds of Papagayo and of the other animals. I made these backgrounds seamless, single-colored so that the animals appeared to have a dimensionality, to come forward from their backgrounds. I also contrasted the animals by depicting them in different textures: Papagayo is very sharply depicted, with bright—sometimes clashing—colors to represent his personality. He's placed in front of the white background, which makes him stand out more. The night creatures don't dominate any of the pages like he does. They're muted. The colors reflect the vivid Amazonian rainforest setting, the personality of the hero, and the contrasts and conflicts.

Engagement Activities

During a **first reading**, it is mainly important that listeners and viewers experience the character of Papagayo and the contrasts, conflicts, and tensions embodied in the narrative.

Have the students look carefully at the title and the illustrations of the cover. Ask if anyone knows what the word *Papagayo* means. (It is Portuguese for "parrot"). Invite individuals to suggest adjectives that they think *might* be appropriate to describe the bird's character. What is there about the title and cover illustration that suggested these adjectives? Keep a list of the words and return to it after a first reading to see which of them were appropriate. As the children look at the endpapers, title, and copyright and dedication pages, they can make predictions about what elements—settings, characters, and actions—might occur in the story.

During a first reading, do not comment, but do invite listeners and viewers to interrupt, make notes, or remember whenever they notice a conflict. These responses can be recorded, and after the first reading they can be discussed. After the reading, the character adjectives can be discussed. Children can explain which words should be left on the list and why, which should be deleted, and which new words should be added. The adjectives from the revised list can be added to the "Dictionary of Character and Emotions."

Before beginning a **second reading**, reintroduce the list of conflicts the children noticed during and after the first reading. Discuss the idea of resolution, the overcoming or solving of conflicts. As you reread the story, have the students look for resolutions—if, when, and how these happen. After the reading, children can be asked if any of the conflicts have been completely resolved. They may notice that Papagayo hasn't given up his raucous, mischievous behavior and that—as the bird warns the night creatures—the monster dog will be back. Older students may wish to discuss what these incomplete resolutions reflect about life. One possibility is that balance and control, in individual lives and within groups, is often very tenuous and that these qualities can only be maintained through constant work.

After a second reading, students can discuss the contrasts in the personalities of Papagayo and the night people. He has both faults and virtues, as do they. Indeed, his raucous vitality is both negative (when it is used to annoy others) and positive (when it is used to help them). The creatures are quiet and gentle, but they are also timid and indecisive at first, and later, they give themselves more credit than they deserve. Students can discuss reasons for the success of the counteroffensive against the dog, noticing the interdependence and cooperation exhibited by Papagayo and the others. These qualities can be considered symbolic of social, group success, and also of a healthy, integrated personality.

A **third reading** can focus on how the illustrations communicate characterization, conflict, and theme. Viewers should notice the use of color, design, and detail within and between pictures. In the first three pictures, Papagayo's vitality is suggested not only by the vivid hues but also by the fact that he seems in constant motion, even when perched on a branch. The night creatures are below him and seem confused and, as their eyes and body language indicate, alarmed and annoyed by his actions. At night, when they are active, their motions don't seem as vigorous as Papagayo's were.

The dominance of the monster dog over the creatures and its power early in the conflict is reflected by its position above them and its increasing size. The postures and expressions of the night creatures indicate their continuing timidity. Notice that, on successive pages, the animals show increasing alarm, but they do not do anything. Viewers can look for a picture that reveals that the dog will not destroy the moon. When Papagayo appears—the first time that he is seen awake at night—he is larger than his enemy and is facing the dog directly.

Viewers can notice how, as the parrot organizes the animals, they are placed higher in the pictures, become more active, and wear happier expressions. The double-spread depicting their driving the monster dog away reveals the degree of harmony and cooperation they have achieved. They form a kind of crescent around the crescent moon. Papagayo does not dominate the scene as he had earlier ones. The dog, defeated, is smaller. Victory achieved, the close relationship among the animals quickly breaks up. Papagayo is on one side of the page; the night people—none of whom is looking at the bird—are congratulating each other and wearing self-satisfied expressions. After looking at the final illustration, which is quite similar to the first one, viewers can ask, "How much has changed in the story?"

Extension Activities

Literature: Have the students look at the second-to-last picture, in which the crescent moon holds the outline of the full moon. Ask them what the moon will look like in another fourteen days and then each day after that. The moon will be full and then will start to wane again. In the story, what will cause the waning? Have the children notice that each time there is a full moon, the monster dog will start eating it and the night creatures and Papagayo will have to chase the dog away so that the moon can begin to regenerate. This is a make-believe story, but in it McDermott offers an imaginary explanation about the cycles of the moon.

Ask the students if they remember the term used to identify stories that explain why and how things came to be the way they are. These are called pourquoi stories. Children can then recall other pourquoi stories. They may know McDermott's *Anansi the Spider* (which explains how the moon got into the sky), *Jabutí the Tortoise*, and *Raven. Architect of the Moon* (by Tim Wynne-Jones, illustrated by Ian Wallace) is another imaginary explanation of the moon's cycles. Children may enjoy noticing the similarities and, more important, the differences between the characters, events, and conflicts of the two stories.

After discussing the theme of cooperation between a "different" individual and a group, readers can relate their observations to McDermott's *Anansi the Spider, Arrow to the Sun, Jabutí the Tortoise,* and *Coyote.* They can also compare and contrast Papagayo to the helper figures in *Raven, Arrow to the Sun,* and *Anansi the Spider.*

Unlike most of McDermott's stories, this one doesn't specify the culture group or geographical area from which the story derives. The children can engage in detective work to suggest a location. First, they can make a list of the animals in the story and find where they come from. Then they can notice where very bright, colorful flowers can be found, along with ruins like those where the monster dog sleeps. They should then look up the word *Papagayo*, discovering what language it is from. With this list compiled, they can locate which single area (Brazilian rainforest) is most often represented in the list. This would be the best possible (hypothetical) region for the story.

Having located the Amazonian rainforest, students can look for other stories centered there and can read a number of these to see how they reveal or reflect the cultural beliefs and values of the people who tell them. Among interesting retellings are *Tales from the Amazon* (adapted by Martin Elbl and J. T. Winik), *Feathers like a Rainbow: An Amazon Indian Tale* (by Flora), *The Great Kapok Tree: A Tale of the Amazon Rain Forest* (by Lynne Cherry), *Tales of a Trickster Guinea Pig: Zorro and Quwi* (by Rebecca Hickox), and *Jabutí the Tortoise* (by McDermott).

Bird stories are important in cultures around the world. In addition to *Feathers like a Rainbow* and McDermott's *Raven* and *Coyote*, children may enjoy Virginia Hamilton's *When Birds Could Talk & Bats Could Sing* and Tololwa Mollel's *A Promise to the Sun*.

Language Arts: During the story, Papagayo cries out, "Craawk! Cra-caocao-cao!" The night creatures, scaring the monster dog, chant, "Chaca-chaca-chaca." In addition to these onomatopoetic sounds, there are many important words in the story that begin with the letter *c*. Among them are *complain, clutching, croon, creep, crumbling, chuckling, crescent, chanting, creatures, chorus, cries, cracked, clucked, comes, curling, color.* Also significant are the small words *can* and *can't*. Write these two words on the board and discuss how they relate to the attitudes and actions of Papagayo and the night creatures. Then give the students a list of the other *c* words. As a group, the class can first discuss the meanings of the words and then how they relate to the characters and events in the story. Students can also suggest other "*c*" words that could apply to the story, including *cooperation* and *cowardice.*

Have the students recall that the story ended without a final, complete resolution to the conflict between the night creatures and the monster dog. They can then brainstorm about what happens over the next month. They should discuss the actions and reactions of the main character (Papagayo, the night creatures, and the monster dog). Here are some items they might wish to discuss. To what extent will the night creatures remember Papagayo's words of warning? How might the conflict between the dog and the forest creatures be more satisfactorily resolved? Will the night creatures change their basic personalities? Will Papagayo ever stop being a mischief-maker? Individual students can use the results of the class brainstorming as materials for the writing of a sequel.

The Arts: Edward Barnes has made *Papagayo* into a short puppet opera. Details are available on line at www.edbarnes.com. Students may wish to visit this site for ideas about staging their own dramatic or puppet version of the story. As this is one of the few McDermott stories that do not include logos for specific characters, students might wish to create their own logos for the parrot, night creatures, and dog. These could be used in lieu of costumes in a play about the story.

Social Studies and Science: If the students have looked up where the various animals are from, they may wish to engage in further research about the habitat, behavior patterns, and diets of the various night creatures and Papagayo. These investigations can be complemented with a study of the interrelationships among the different components of a South American rainforest ecosystem. They can also discuss how, just as the monster dog is eating away at the moon, the life of the rainforest is being eaten away by many forces of modern civilization.

References

Cherry, Lynne. *The Great Kapok Tree: A Tale of the Amazon Rain Forest.* San Diego: Gulliver Books, 1990.

Elbl, Martin and J. T. Winik, retellers. Illustrated by Gerda Neubacher. *Tales from the Amazon.* Burlington, Ontario: Hayes Publishing, 1986.

Flora. *Feathers like a Rainbow: An Amazon Indian Tale.* New York: Harper & Row, 1989.

Hamilton, Virginia. Illustrated by Barry Moser. *When Birds Could Talk & Bats Could Sing.* New York: Blue Sky Press, 1996.

Hickox, Rebecca. Illustrated by Kim Howard. *Tales of a Trickster Guinea Pig: Zorro and Quwi.* New York: Doubleday, 1990.

Mollel, Tololwa M. Illustrated by Beatriz Vidal. *A Promise to the Sun.* Boston: Joy Street/ Little Brown, 1992.

Wynne-Jones, Tim. Illustrated by Ian Wallace. *Architect of the Moon.* Toronto: Groundwood, 1988.

DANIEL O'ROURKE
AN IRISH TALE

(1986)

INTRODUCING THE STORY

When Gerald McDermott decided to retell stories from his Irish heritage, he made as his first choice "Daniel O'Rourke," a tale first collected in 1813. Told to Crofton Croker by an old man who claimed to have experienced the events several decades earlier, it involved the old man's being carried by an eagle to the moon, later being dumped into the sea by a flock of geese, and then carried about suspended in the spout of a whale. Both the character and the plot—including a sky flight and fall—appealed to McDermott.

McDermott altered the story, removing the frame narrative in which a garrulous old man tried to convince his listener of the truth of his story, leaving out the "red nosed" old man's references to his having had too much to drink the night of his adventure, changing the time of the story from Lady-Day (the Vernal Equinox) to Midsummer Night, and softening the cranky personality of Daniel. These changes make McDermott's telling focus directly on the events and Daniel's role in them, rather than making it appear as the fabricated tale of a man who knew how to incorporate the Celtic tale-type of abduction by fairies into a yarn that brought a degree of notoriety to the teller and free drinks for his efforts. The placing of the story at Midsummer Night under a full moon,

Daniel O'Rourke stepped out into the
night, passed through the great stone gates
of the mansion, and walked down the
hill toward the little white cottage where
he lived with his mother. Dan paused
for a moment by the pooka spirit's tower,
stretched, yawned, and then continued
on his way. Just as he was about to cross
the brook, he looked up and saw all the
stars in the summer sky.
   "Lovely," he said.

times when mischievous spirits were known to be especially active, makes Daniel
more culpable for his misfortunes. He would have known about the dangers of
that night and, therefore, should have been more cautious.

The opening pages of the picture book merely state the facts of the early
part of Daniel's night out: he arrives at the great mansion, dances, eats, and
then heads home alone. Only three phrases imply that he may be heading for
trouble. His dining "until he thought he would burst" indicates his gluttony,
while the references to a "fine summer evening" and "the pooka spirit's tower"
that he stops by on the way home suggest that trouble could be coming from beings who are, as McDermott states in his introductory note, "responsible . . . for
much of the capricious mischief that befalls ordinary folk."

The illustrations reveal much more about Daniel's character failings and the
possible dangers he faces. On the title page, he is depicted taking great care in
grooming and dressing himself, and he looks very pleased with himself. His clothing, a clashing combination of purple, green, brown, and red plaid, sets him
apart from the liveried butlers and well-dressed upper-class guests. However, he

dominates the scenes in which he dances and eats, apparently oblivious to others, including the servants who look askance as he overloads three plates at the buffet table. Unbeknown to him, three tiny, green-clad leprechauns lurk by the food dishes, and as he walks jauntily home, the little people hide by the ruined tower. The danger of the scene is increased by the fact that the moon is full. Egotistical, gluttonous, and oblivious to danger, Daniel O'Rourke is courting disaster.

During the wild sequence of events that follow, Daniel is depicted as small and humble in the pictures. He sits meekly before a giant eagle, clings precariously to a reaping-rod sticking from the moon, falls head-over-heels downward, and flounders on a whale's spout. The events link his misfortunes to earlier behavior: he had robbed the eagle's nest, dined on goose-liver pate, and nibbled cheese that is the same color as the moon. As he plummets to the ocean floor, he is watched by a startled lobster not unlike the one seen on the buffet table. It would appear that Daniel is being punished because of his excesses and misdeeds.

The interplay between the words and pictures of the last few pages gives rise to questions about the nature of Daniel's adventures and the extent of his resolution to reform. In the text, his mother, who has thrown a bucket of water in his face, scolds him for foolishly falling asleep under a pooka tower, and Daniel, we are told, never again robbed an eagle's nest, ate green cheese or goose liver, or slept under a pooka tower. In the penultimate illustration, Daniel looks bewildered; two goose feathers lie on the ground beside him; the three tiny leprechauns look on gleefully; beside them is the ghostly form of a nightmare. Did the leprechauns induce the dream, or was it a result of his overeating? And where did the goose feathers come from? Did the events actually occur? Significantly, Daniel does not offer any elaboration on his agreement with his mother's statement, "You've had no easy rest of it, I'm sure." Is he embarrassed, ashamed, or just uncertain?

In the final illustration, Daniel has again become the largest figure on the page. One of the goose quills has literally become a feather in his cap. As he holds the other, he smiles, looking at it and winking at the same time. With his left hand, he grips the edge of his coat in what appears to be a thumbs-up gesture. Is his ego reasserting itself , and has what appeared to be a journey of humiliation turned into one of which he is secretly proud and delighted? Is he sharing a knowing wink with the audience, indicating that although he may not fall asleep again under a pooka tower, he is undoubtedly going to get into more mischief? Like Coyote, he may have a nose for trouble.

THE AUTHOR DISCUSSES THE STORY

Although I hadn't been to Ireland when I did this book (just as I hadn't been to the Pueblos when I did *Arrow to the Sun*), I had always felt connected to Ireland through my grandparents, who were of Irish origin. And so, after writing books about so many different world traditions, I decided to make a direct link with my own ancestors. Doing the book was a way of achieving this. I think that's why I created a caricature of myself to represent Daniel. It was a way of putting myself into the mythical landscape of my ancestors.

When I was reading an early nineteenth-century collection of Irish folktales, the story leapt out at me. It had all the wonderful elements of a crazy dream; it was a fantastical journey in the extreme; and I'd wanted to create a light-hearted story—it was ideal. And, in a way, I saw in O'Rourke a person who reminded me a bit of some aspects in myself. In the original version of the story, he used a great many elements of Celtic folklore to tell a story that he said was about himself. In a way, I use traditional motifs to present characters whose lives strike a deep inner chord with me. So that may be another reason that he looks like me in the illustrations.

The original version was very long, far too long for a picture book, so I pared the narrative down. I wanted to get to the heart of the story about how this man comes in contact with very powerful magical forces but isn't able to connect with them. It's midsummer night and a full moon, and the forces are there; but he doesn't profit from the experience. In the pictures, I used deep green colors to symbolize the world of the soul or the spirit. Daniel never becomes a part of it. I deliberately made his clothes a hodge-podge of styles and colors to suggest his sense of confusion about where he is and who he is in life. In many ways, I wanted to create a deliberate ambiguity at the end. I played the matter-of-fact statements of the prose against the fantasy element of the adventure. Did the events really happen? There are hints that they may have; but that's not stated. Did Daniel reform? I doubt it.

In creating the art work, I drew on both old and new styles. I tried to give the pictures a sense of having aged of having come from the early nineteenth century, along with the story. But I used many different angles for viewing events. I wanted to be more cinematic, to work in a different way from the flat, two-dimensional style of many of my earlier works.

Engagement Activities

Begin a **first reading** by having the students notice the dominant color of the story. Ask them to be on the lookout for the use of that color during the story. Ask them to see if there are any possible conflicts suggested by the cover illustration. One way to facilitate this discussion is to ask what different kinds of "beings" are depicted. What kinds of conflicts are frequently found in stories with human beings and magical little people?

Students can continue their predictions by studying the illustrations on the title and dedication pages and the first page of the story. They might consider what Daniel is doing on the title page, how well or poorly coordinated his wardrobe is, what the old lady (his mother) thinks about his going somewhere, the contrasts between his house and the mansion, and the fact that there is a full moon on Midsummer Night. The pictures of Daniel's entrance into the party, his dancing, and his eating also contain details that reflect elements of his character and others' reactions. Give the students opportunity to study the buffet table, allowing them to notice on their own the three "wee" folk. After finishing these pictures they can suggest other possible conflicts. Read the story through and then ask the students which of the predicted conflicts occurred and which new ones they noticed.

Before the **second reading**, ask students to recall elements of the plot, including the actions in the preliminary pages. Note these on the board, along with others they may not have recalled. Then work with the students to arrange these in chronological order. During the rereading the students should look carefully at the pictures and listen carefully to the words so that they can keep a record of how Daniel acts and reacts in each situation. For example, they can see that he likes to be the center of attention and looks very pleased with himself while he is dancing. When the eagle leaves him hanging on the moon, Daniel bawls and calls him "a beast and a brute." At the end, he makes a promise, but he winks and doesn't look at his mother. These actions and reactions can be recorded next to the appropriate events. Students can then discuss whether or not there is something about Daniel's behavior and attitude that makes him responsible for the conflicts in which he finds himself.

Students can finally discuss the ambiguity of the ending, focusing on two questions: "Did the events really happen? Does Daniel become a better person because of what he's learned from his experience?" Students can notice that the events and characters of his fantastic journey relate to aspects of his waking world, as is generally the case in dream-journey stories. However, when he falls from the sky, he is clutching goose feathers, two of which are found in the last two pictures when he is definitely awake. Does he, in the last picture, look repentant, or does he seem to be reverting to the egotistical individual he was? Discuss the saying "a feather in your cap," and note that this is where Daniel has stuck one. And why is he facing toward the reader instead of following his mother home?

A **third reading** can focus on McDermott's use of color, particularly green, and the size and position of the central character in each illustration and can relate these aspects to plot, conflict, and character development. Show the students the difference between the green hue of Daniel's coat and the green of the "wee folk" and shamrocks on the title page. Explain that McDermott used the deep green colors to symbolize the world of nature and the supernatural. How well does Daniel fit into these worlds? What do the clashing colors of his outfit suggest about his character and his relationship with the green world? Is it significant that he seems most at home when he's in a world with many different colors? Have the students relate how Daniel feels about himself and his situation to how large and dominant he is in the illustrations.

Extension Activities

Literature: "What goes up must come down." This simple statement about the law of gravity applies to Daniel O'Rourke and several other McDermott characters who ascend and descend, both literally and symbolically. Students can compare Daniel to Coyote and Icarus (*Sunflight*), each of whom falls from the sky because of character flaws. Both Daniel and Jabutí are released by birds, but whereas the latter is betrayed, the former is dropped as a punishment for his misdeeds. Daniel's descent can be contrasted to those of the Boy (*Arrow to the Sun*) and Wind (*Musicians of the Sun*), who travel from the Sun to the Earth with boons for human beings.

Daniel's moonlit Midsummer Night adventures into the realm of the supernatural serve as a punishment, one he may or may not learn from. Students may enjoy three other stories in which the central characters enter enchanted Celtic realms: *The Woman Who Flummoxed the Fairies* (Heather Forest), *The Nightwood* (Robin Muller), and *The Willow Maiden* (Megan Collins). Each of the central characters passes a series of dangerous tests and returns home positively changed as a result of the adventures. Students can study these stories, discussing how the strengths of character these people possess enable them to complete successfully their circular journeys.

If the story is seen as a dream, it can be compared to both Maurice Sendak's *Where the Wild Things Are* and Chris Van Allsburg's *Just a Dream*. In both of these stories, aspects of the waking world appear in the dream world and relate to the conflicts the characters resolve. They awaken changed, with more positive attitudes, something, it could be argued, that is not the case for Daniel.

Language Arts: The three leprechauns are not mentioned in the text, which focuses on Daniel; and in the four pictures in which they do appear, they are behind him. He neither sees them nor seems to be aware of their presence. This seems to be their intention; they are acting on him without his knowledge. After brainstorming, students can write dialogue for each of the three wee folk for the pre- and post-adventure illustrations in which they appear. Some prewriting questions students might consider: Why do they first appear at the buffet table? What might they be thinking as Daniel loads up his plates? What are they saying as they see Daniel striding toward the bridge? What are they planning and why? What are they doing as Daniel crosses the bridge? Is the shillelagh being used as a kind of magic wand? As they hide behind the wall, what do they think about (and maybe later say) about Daniel's predicament?

Referring to the earlier compiled list of events and Daniel's responses, students can discuss his character and emotions and enter the words into the "Dictionary of Character and Emotions."

Social Studies: The story reflects the social structure of early Nineteenth-century Ireland. Daniel, a poor man, leaves his simple home to attend a banquet at the grand home of one of the rich people (who may have been English). Students can study the types of homes these two different classes would have lived in at the time. The students could notice the different clothing the people wear. Daniel's seems to consist of mismatched castoffs, with, as the later illustrations reveal, loose buttons. They could then try to identify the foods Daniel is enjoying and consider why these items would not have been part of his regular diet. What would he usually have eaten?

The party is probably part of a Midsummer Night festival. What were some of the customs observed by the Irish on that occasion? What were some of the folk beliefs about that day of which Daniel ought to have been aware when he decided to go home alone?

The Arts: Both the cover and the scene of Daniel performing in the ballroom emphasize the importance of music and dance in the story and, by extension, in Irish life, particularly in earlier times. Students may enjoy listening to Irish folk songs and simple dance tunes and perhaps may even attempt to perform some of them. They might also consider whether the rich people would be performing different dances, perhaps those fashionable in England or on the continent. A video of traditional Irish dances would provide an interesting complement to the study of the story.

References

Collins, Megan. Illustrated by Laszlo Gal. *The Willow Maiden.* New York: Dial Books, 1985.

Forest, Heather. Illustrated by Susan Carter. *The Woman Who Flummoxed the Fairies.* San Diego: Harcourt, Brace, Jovanovich, 1988.

Muller, Robin. *The Nightwood.* Toronto: Doubleday Canada, 1991.

Sendak, Maurice. *Where the Wild Things Are.* New York: Harper & Row, 1963.

Van Allsburg, Chris. *Just a Dream.* Boston: Houghton Mifflin, 1990.

ZOMO THE RABBIT
A TRICKSTER TALE FROM WEST AFRICA

(1992)

INTRODUCING THE STORY

Along with Tortoise and Anansi the Spider, Hare or Rabbit is one of the most popular trickster figures of sub-Saharan Africa, especially in Nigeria. Like animal tricksters found around the world, he is both clever and self-centered. The latter quality frequently lands him in trouble. Tales of Rabbit, along with those of Spider, traveled aboard slave ships to the Caribbean and North America, where the small characters' adventures were adapted to reflect conditions of a people repressed by powerful masters. Brer Rabbit, whose escapades were first made famous by the later-Nineteenth-century writer Joel Chandler Harris, is the best-known example of the African turned American trickster-rabbit.

The first of the four trickster tales McDermott retold and illustrated between 1992 and 2002, *Zomo* focuses on a character who, even though he interacts with other beings, including some who live above the earth, is a solitary figure. Although his deeds sometimes benefit others, he is concerned with fulfilling his own needs and desires. In this case, the trickster is on a quest—not to acquire a physical object or to achieve a physical competency, or to be presented

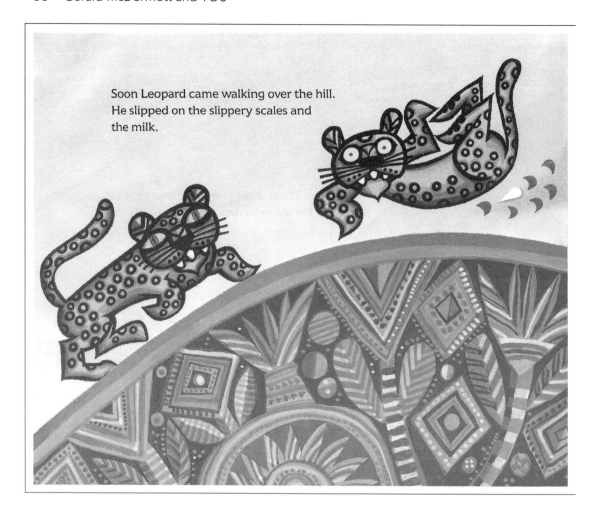

Soon Leopard came walking over the hill. He slipped on the slippery scales and the milk.

a ceremony—but to become the possessor of an abstract quality: wisdom. In the story, wisdom is presented as something different from cleverness—which the rabbit already exhibits.

As the Sky God explains when Zomo makes his request, the rabbit must earn the prize and, like many questers in folklore, he must perform three impossible tasks. Much of the picture book explains how Zomo is able to overcome great, seemingly insurmountable odds to achieve success. In exchange for three objects, the Sky God gives advice, explaining that although Zomo has "lots of courage, [and] a bit of sense, [he has] no caution." The deity's advice is to use speed to escape the angry animals he had humiliated during his request. The book's conclusion seems to imply that, given his character, Zomo will, in the future, have to use his wisdom frequently to tell him when he must use his speed to escape from those he annoys with his selfish tricks.

The colors of green and yellow, suggesting the equatorial jungles that provide the setting for the story, dominate the gouache on watercolor paper illustrations. Their vividness also reinforces the vitality of the central character, who

He rolled down the hill.

wears a brightly colored African shirt and hat. He is in motion in thirteen of the fifteen illustrations, another suggestion of his irrepressible character. In the final picture, he appears to be leaping off the page, bounding, no doubt, toward a new mischief-filled adventure.

Interestingly, the three animals whom Zomo encounters on his quest are depicted on the Sky God's robe, as are the objects the rabbit takes from them. The Sky God does not need what he asks Zomo to bring him. In his power, he releases them to test the rabbit's ability to get and then return them. Perhaps the animals themselves are allowed to remain behind on earth because the Sky God knows that Zomo will always need to be reminded of the components and uses of wisdom.

THE AUTHOR DISCUSSES THE STORY

When I was making animated films, I was very interested in the art and design of work from West Africa, particularly the textiles of the Ashanti, Yoruba, and Hausa peoples. The traditional arts were very symbolic and stylized, something that interested me because of my training in graphic design. I linked the two in *Anansi*. But in later years I became interested in other styles.

In 1992, when Harcourt Brace invited me to do a series of trickster books, I thought of both West African design and West African trickster stories. The rabbit appealed to me personally; in a way I saw his position as being a little like mine as an artist. He was not getting a lot of notice and he had to use his wits to survive. I wouldn't call him a role model; but something about his character called to me. I was also interested in Zomo because of all the rabbit stories that enslaved Africans brought with them to America. He's the ancestor of Brer Rabbit in the southern United States and Compere Lupin in the Caribbean.

My research into the textiles and clothing had a strong influence on how I used illustrations to communicate the themes of the story. I incorporated into the Sky God's robes the objects of the rabbit's quest and the design patterns for the landscape. The Sky God was the creator; all of the things in Zomo's world came from him. The landscape is deliberately stylized to link it back to its source. I used very limited color, as I have for all my trickster stories: yellow-gold to represent the tropical heat and green for the lush vegetation. Communicating a sense of movement was also important. Zomo had to know when to be still and when to get going. The pictures show both of these.

Engagement Activities

Before a **first reading**, have the students discuss the meanings of the words *cleverness* and *wisdom*. They should notice that having the first quality does not guarantee possession of the second. In upper elementary grades, students can provide examples of behaviors that are clever and those that are wise. They might also provide examples of contemporary historical or fictional characters who are wise or clever. Explain that these two qualities will be important in the story about to be read.

Have the students look carefully at the front cover, noticing the subtitle and the depiction of the central character. Ask them if they remember any other trickster stories and stories about rabbits. After listing their responses, have the students predict how and why the words *cleverness* and *wisdom* might be important to this story. They can then hypothesize on what the conflicts in the story might be, using their background literary knowledge, their awareness of the two character traits, and their remembrance of details on the cover. Note down the students' responses.

On a first reading, go through the story giving the children plenty of time to look at each picture. After the reading, ask the students which of their conflict predictions were accurate. Have them see that it was the knowledge and information they brought to these predictions that helped them when they made correct assumptions. Discuss the terms *cleverness* and *wisdom* as they apply to Zomo and his actions in the story. Does he possess more of one than the other? At the end of the story, how wise is he really? Remind the students to refer to specific details (visual and verbal) from the story.

Before a **second reading**, review with the students the general concept of story conflict: a problem at or near the beginning that isn't usually resolved until the end. It is what the character or characters do in the middle of the story that brings about (or fails to bring about) the resolution. How generally might a trickster resolve conflicts? Students can note that by being clever, by using his wits, by trickery, this type of character is frequently (although not always) successful.

Ask the students to notice the conflicts and steps toward resolution as you reread the story. After the reading, discuss the initial conflict (Zomo doesn't have and wants wisdom) and how the rabbit initially tries to resolve the problem (by asking for, not by earning or working for, wisdom). What new conflict does the Sky God introduce? He asks the rabbit to do "three impossible things." Students can discuss why these tasks appear impossible for Zomo to perform, how he solves the problems and overcomes the obstacles, and, finally, why the Sky God had demanded that these tasks be successfully completed before he granted the trickster's request. These answers should consider to what extent and how Zomo acquired wisdom. In what ways do the final words of the Sky God represent wisdom? Do the students think that Zomo really gains wisdom, and why or why not?

Students can enter appropriate words in their "Dictionary of Character and Emotions."

During a **third reading**, students can focus on the visual elements of the book. They can be invited to look for the dominant colors in the book as a whole and on each page, the position and size of the rabbit in the illustrations, the emotions revealed by each character, and, finally, the differences in the Sky God's garments earlier and later in the story. Why do the earlier pictures display the animals and items requested, whereas the later ones do not? As noted, much of the story involves motion. Students can discuss why it is sometimes important for Zomo to remain still and why he should sometimes move.

Interestingly, the expression of each of the tricked characters changes during the tricking. Students can suggest what changing emotions these expressions reveal. Finally, students can notice the symbol on the title page. Because it is not as character specific as other McDermott symbols, they can examine it in relation to the visual details in the book and then suggest its significance.

Extension Activities

Literature: Zomo's character invites comparison with other McDermott trickster figures. Students can see in what ways the rabbit's character and actions are similar to and different from those of Raven, Coyote, and Jabutí. Like Coyote, he seems to have a nose for trouble; in this story at least, his actions do not benefit others, whereas those of Raven and Jabutí do. However, like Raven, he must use cleverness and deception to achieve his goals, and, like those of Jabutí and Coyote, some of his actions have annoyed others. He is certainly as self-centered as Papagayo, Coyote, and Daniel O'Rourke.

Zomo's adventures can be compared with those of the other well-known African tricksters, Anansi and Tortoise. In Gail Haley's *A Story, a Story*, the Ashanti trickster Anansi also approaches the Sky God with a request and is assigned three seemingly impossible tasks. Students can compare the motivations of the two tricksters and examine the strategies each uses to achieve his ends. Verna Aardema's *Who's in Rabbit's House* provides an interesting story in which the trickster is out-tricked by a lesser figure.

Zomo can also be compared to his North American descendent Brer Rabbit, whose adventures have recently been retold by Julius Lester in *The Tales of Uncle Remus: The Adventures of Brer Rabbit*. Priscilla Jaquith's *Bo Rabbit Smart for True: Folktales from the Gullah* is a collection from the coastal areas of George and South Carolina. Told as they were by once-enslaved people, these tales can be compared to similar ones told in Africa. The differences in events and characterization will reflect the differing social conditions out of which the stories emerged. Many rabbit stories from Africa seem to have blended with trickster tales of the Cherokee peoples of North Carolina and Georgia and with stories from other southeastern Native groups. Many of these have been collected and retold by Cherokee author Gayle Ross in *How Rabbit Tricked Otter and other Cherokee Trickster Stories*.

Language Arts: Among the abstract terms used in the story are "clever," "wisdom," "earn," "courage," and "caution." After reviewing how these words are used in the narrative, introduce the terms "deception," "enticement," "insult," "request," "irresistible," and "challenge"—which are not found in the text. These terms can be discussed and students can suggest if and how they might be applied to situations and characters in the story.

Ask the students to study carefully one of the double-spreads in the story, noticing how color, details, and picture design are used to depict actions, conflicts, and character not presented or not presented in detail by the verbal text. The students can then be given the task of creating an extended verbal text of narrative and description for one double-spread. This is the kind of narrative and description the author might have used if he hadn't had the visual text to communicate a great deal of his meaning.

When Zomo receives advice about wisdom from the Sky God, the question is, "Will he use it wisely and how?" Have the students create a difficult situation that the rabbit could find himself in. They can consider to what extent he is responsible for his predicament. Is he in it because he used or failed to use his wisdom? How might he use wisdom to get out of the difficult situation?

Social Studies: As usual, McDermott's illustrations are based on extensive research into the culture. In this case, Zomo's clothing is based on Hausa styles and designs. His cap is a fila and his shirt, a buba. Clothing in traditional Nigerian culture was seen as an expression of an individual's personality. Students can research traditional clothing, finding examples of styles and designs not unlike those on rabbit's clothes. They can then notice the unique designs on Zomo's attire and discuss how these are reflections of his personality. Interestingly, the Sky God wears the ceremonial agbada, a more formal robe with longer, fuller sleeves.

Students can find out about the roles and uses of the various kinds of drums in traditional Nigerian culture. Drums were used for communication and in ceremonies. They were also used to accompany storytelling and, of course, dancing. One of the jokes in the story is that Zomo is such a skillful drummer that he is able to lure the fish—who can't resist dancing to the rhythm—out of its natural element. Students can search for recordings of contemporary and traditional drum music to try to find a piece that could be enticing enough to lure a fish out of the water.

The Arts: Using the results of their research into traditional Nigerian arts (music, clothing, and dance), students can prepare a pantomime version of the story. They can create simple designs to be taped or pinned onto T-shirts or made into simple hats and take turns as the various characters dancing out the various events of the story. Appropriate drum music could be played in the background.

References

Aardema, Verna, reteller. Illustrated by Leo and Diane Dillon. *Who's in Rabbit's House.* New York: Dial, 1977.

Haley, Gail, reteller and illustrator. *A Story, a Story.* New York: Antheneum, 1970.

Jaquith, Priscilla, reteller. Illustrated by Ed Young. *Bo Rabbit Smart for True: Folktales from the Gullah.* New York: Philomel, 1981.

Lester, Julius, reteller. Illustrated by Jerry Pinkney. *The Tales of Uncle Remus: The Adventures of Brer Rabbit.* New York: Dial, 1987.

Ross, Gayle, reteller. Illustrated by Murv Jacob. *How Rabbit Tricked Otter and Other Cherokee Trickster Stories.* New York: HarperCollins, 1994.

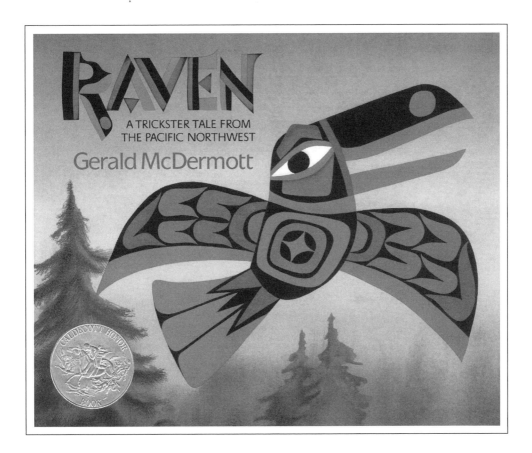

RAVEN
A TRICKSTER TALE FROM THE PACIFIC NORTHWEST

(1993)

INTRODUCING THE STORY

Raven is the central figure in the mythology of the Tsimsham, Tlingit, and Haida peoples of the Northwest Coast. Clever, sometimes helpful, but frequently selfish, he has many roles: culture-hero, trickster, transformer, creator. Some of the traditional Raven stories provided comic instruction and delight; however, others were considered extremely serious. The best known of the tales–the account of his finding the sun and bringing it to the people—is of the latter type. Some versions of this pourquoi myth also explain how the bird—which was originally white—acquired its present color. Many scholars have seen the myth as a highly significant account of how the world was transformed—symbolically, as well as literally—into its present state.

McDermott's adaptation follows the basic outline of the legend. Flying through the darkness, Raven notices the suffering of the people and decides to search for light. When he discovers it in the home of the Sky Chief, he transforms himself into a pine needle that the chief's daughter swallows. Raven is thus born as a baby boy who demands to be allowed to play with the boxes in which the Sky Chief has confined the sun. His wishes granted, he morphs into his bird form, seizes the sun in his beak, and flies with it back to this world, where he releases the orb into the sky.

Sky Chief, his daughter, and the elders looked on in amazement. Raven plucked up the ball of light in his beak, flew through the smoke hole of the lodge, and disappeared into the dark sky.

In addition to its accurate depiction of the physical and cultural elements of the West Coast peoples, McDermott's picture book reflects the author's interest in the power of myth to mediate between extremes and to present ways of achieving unity and completion within both individuals and societies. In his illustrations, McDermott uses the bold designs and vivid colors of traditional Northwest Coast art. The sharply defined, abstract designs that depict Raven are contrasted with the more realistic depictions of the human figures and the landscape. These contrasts distinguish Raven from his surroundings and emphasize his centrality in the story. Like other McDermott characters, the hero also wears a symbol that is appropriate for his role in the story, representing as it does the sun that had been contained within the stacking boxes.

The hero's transformation of the landscape is revealed partly through the use of color. The dreariness and indistinctness of the countryside at the beginning reflects the physical and emotional states of the people. The darkness is contrasted with the yellow-gold colors that dominate the Sky Chief's lodge. The final illustrations suggest a reconciliation of the extremes, a resolution of the

conflict. The green of the forest does not disappear, and the gold-yellow colors of the sky do not dominate. The two balance and complement each other, a reflection of the fact that Raven has succeeded as a mediator between the two worlds.

THE AUTHOR DISCUSSES THE STORY

At the time I chose (or was chosen by!) the Raven story, I felt that my artistic energies were reemerging. I was transforming, just as Raven does. I was spreading my wings, and I wanted to bring my new work to people as a gift. So Raven was a metaphor for me as an artist, a storyteller, seeking light and then sharing it. Raven has the energy of my other tricksters, and he's full of mischief. But he has a divine quality as well; he can enter into the sky world and transform our world. He's also a bit of a rebel: he fights the established order of the Sky Chief so that the deprived people on Earth can enhance their lives. But you get the idea that he still has fun doing all this; he enjoys his mischief making.

In order to depict the two worlds of the story and the change that takes place, I chose to use two art styles. Watercolor washes depict the wet, cloudy landscape of the Northwest Coast. The dominant colors of grey and blue early in the story suggest a world in the formative stages, one without the gift of light. The world of the Sky Chief has warm tones, yellows, and golds. This is the divine world; it has what the human world lacks. By the end of the story, the colors of the two worlds are interrelated.

To emphasize Raven's character, particularly his uniqueness in his world, I employed more vivid, bright colors. I combined the bold designs and colors I'd learned in my graphic arts studies and combined them with the sharply defined qualities found in Northwest Coast art, particularly the representation of figures on totem poles. I wanted to show that even though Raven had links to both worlds in the story, he was unique. I wanted readers to get a sense of this and of his hard-edged, spiky character as well.

To my delight, when the Tlingit community began a program of translating children's books into their own language, the first title they chose was *Raven*.

Engagement Activities

Before a **first reading**, have students look carefully at the front cover, noticing first the title, subtitle, and author; then, the foreground figure; and, finally, the background. From what they know about story structure and how illustrations work, they can make some preliminary predictions about the story, particularly possible conflicts, the name and nature of the main character, and the setting—and possibly how these three aspects are related. If they are familiar with other McDermott books, trickster stories, Northwest Coast landscape, and Native culture, they can use this knowledge to expand on their predictions. Then, have them look at the illustration on the back cover. What is the difference? The bird is basically the same; however, the sky is lighter and bluer. When the students notice this difference, they can further expand on their predictions. After looking at the preliminary material, especially the dedication page, they can discuss the symbol and link it to Raven. In reading the story and viewing the illustrations, they should be looking at details that may help to explain the appropriateness of the logo.

During the first reading, pause before turning each page and invite students to interrupt when and if they observe any conflicts. Quickly note each observation on the board. After the reading, discuss the list of conflicts and add any others you or they may suggest. Some conflicts include the lack of light, the effect of this lack on the lives of the people, Raven's sadness at the situation, the problems of getting into the Sky Chief's lodge, of acquiring the sun, and of escaping with it. Students can then discuss how Raven resolves the conflicts, examining his creative problem solving, that is, his using tricks to fulfill his objectives. They can then discuss whether or not they feel that the theft was a justifiable, morally correct action. Finally, the students can consider the appropriateness of Raven's symbol.

A **second reading** can focus on how the illustrations reveal the introduction, development, and resolution of the conflicts. Begin by looking again at the front and back covers, discussing the ways they reveal the situation at the beginning and end of the story. Viewers can then look page by page at the colors, discussing how these indicate stages in the conflict. Notice the movement from dark blues and greens to increasing, almost too intense, yellows and oranges, to a more balanced array of colors at the conclusion. Discuss the way McDermott uses colors and color changes to reflect the conflicts between opposites—dark–light, night–day, sky–earth—and the nature of the reconciliation Raven brings about.

Students can then contrast two sets of pictures: two of Raven with the people's village below him and two of him either entering or exiting the Sky Chief's house. In the first illustration of the first set, they might discuss Raven's worried look, the indistinctness of the village, and the absence of the sun. The fact that Raven is only partly on the page might suggest a lack of completeness and harmony in the world. In the book's last illustration, the village is very distinct, Raven is more centered on the page and is basically midway between the sun and the village. He's a kind of intermediary. It is interesting to note the use of orange on the fish—the only time that color is used on objects away from the Sky Chief's house. In comparing the second set, the children can suggest the significance of the following details: that Raven enters from the left and exits to the right, that he is larger in the exit picture, that the sun in the second picture is released from his beak, and that now more details of the landscape can be seen.

After a **third reading**, older students can discuss how various elements in the story embody cultural beliefs of Northwest Coast Native peoples. Ask them to note key characters, settings, and actions as they listen and view. Among elements they might discuss are Raven's ability to transform himself, an indication of the great spirit power the people attributed to this mythological being. The sun, which provided light and warmth in this frequently damp, foggy, and cloudy area, was not just an object in the sky, but a wonderful gift from a supernatural being, Raven. The fact that the people reciprocate with the gift of fish for Raven reflects the importance of reciprocal gift-giving and sharing among the people. This sharing can be contrasted with the Sky Chief's hiding the sun deep inside the boxes. He lets his "grandson" play with it, but he will not share with the human beings, who need its light and warmth to improve the quality of their lives. The fact that Raven must resort to deception and thievery to acquire the sun for the people is both a negative comment on the Sky Chief's selfishness and an indication of Raven's love of playing tricks for his own amusement.

Extension Activities

Literature: When Raven observes the state of the people in the darkness, he remarks, "I will search for light." The verb is the same as that used in the sentence in *Arrow to the Sun* in which the Boy announces his intention to seek for his father. Both stories show many similarities that students may consider. Among these are a search, a transformation, and the sun as the source of the gift brought to the people by the hero. Students should also notice the differences, including the facts that Raven is without a family, that he does not live with the people whom he helps, and that he doesn't have to pass a series of tests. *Musicians of the Sun* also traces a trip to the sun to bring a gift to people in darkness. While it does not have as many similarities to *Raven* as does *Arrow to the Sun*, children will enjoy seeing how the myth from another culture deals with a movement from darkness to light and color.

The story of Raven's recovery of the light has been retold many times by children's authors and illustrators. *How Raven Brought Light to People* (retold by Ann Dixon, illustrated by James Watts) and *Raven's Light: A Myth from the People of the Northwest Coast* (retold by Susan Hand Shetterly, illustrated by Robert Shetterly) are two fairly recent versions. Each includes the basic story outline but adds some details different from those in McDermott's version, and each uses a different artistic style to depict the Northwest Coast setting and Native artifacts. Using McDermott's *Raven* as a point of departure, students can study these versions, noting how the differences in each influence the story's meaning. Haida artist and author Bill Reid includes the tale in his collection *The Raven Steals the Light* (coauthored with Robert Bringhurst). The stories in this book will present older readers with an idea of the range of the trickster-hero's adventures and misadventures.

Christie Harris's *Mouse Woman and the Vanished Princesses* is a collection of retold legends about a tiny supernatural being who played an important role in the lives of the people of the Northwest Coast. The character's actions and personality can be compared to those of Raven.

Language Arts: In the written text, only three words—"sad", "delighted", "amazement"—are used to reflect the feelings and emotional reactions of the various characters. After considering the significance of the different events in the story, students can come up with additional appropriate "emotional" words for the character's responses. One way to assist the students would be to create a list of words—familiar and unfamiliar, relevant and irrelevant—from which they can chose. For example, *happy* and *perplexed* might be appropriate words, whereas *enraged* might not. At this point students can work on their "Dictionary of Character and Emotions."

During the story, Raven only says "I will search for light" and makes a few baby noises. However, he is probably thinking all the time. For each page students can create cartoon-style thought balloons in which they can write Raven's silent reactions about the situation depicted in the illustration.

In the illustrations, the human people and their village are seen only from above. Viewers do not perceive the changes in the story that take place in the village as a result of Raven's action. Students can brainstorm, discussing what the physical world might have looked like to the people before Raven's gift of the sun, how the people perceived and responded to the change, and what land, sea, and sky looked like to them after the sun shone on their world. Each student can then draw on the results of this collective discussion to write a paragraph of description from the people's point of view—before, during, or after the sun's delivery.

Social Studies: In addition to their response to the spirit world, the people of the Northwest Coast responded to weather and the animal and physical aspects of land and sea. Students can research the traditional life of the people, noticing first the physical aspects of the area—geography, zoology, botany, and weather—and then how the people created a lifestyle or culture that enabled them to co-exist in harmony with the world around them. This research could be engaged in concurrently with or just before the writing of the descriptive paragraph discussed earlier.

The Arts: The arts of the Northwest Coast were not intended merely as decoration, recreation, or entertainment. They were highly sophisticated, stylistically intricate expressions of the people's belief in the vital interrelationship between the human, natural, and supernatural worlds. Traditional art as seen on totem poles, canoes, household objects, and clothing can be carefully examined by students, who can engage in research to discover what the art meant both to creators and "viewers." Particular attention should be paid to those images depicting Raven.

Music and dance formed an integral part of the great cultural and religious festivals held at regular intervals during the year. Available videotapes of ceremonies can be played, with students noticing how performance and visual art was combined with spiritual belief and mythical, cultural history.

References

Dixon, Ann, reteller. Illustrated by James Watts. *How Raven Brought Light to the People.* New York: Margaret K. McElderry Books, 1992.

Harris, Christie. Drawings by Douglas Tait. *Mouse Woman and the Vanished Princesses.* Toronto: McClelland and Stewart, 1976.

Reid, Bill, and Robert Bringhurst. *The Raven Steals the Light.* Vancouver: Douglas & McIntyre; Seattle: University of Washington Press, 1984.

Shetterly, Susan Hand, reteller. Illustrated by Robert Shetterly. *Raven's Light: A Myth from the People of the Northwest Coast.* New York: Atheneum, 1991.

COYOTE
A TRICKSTER TALE FROM THE AMERICAN SOUTHWEST

(1994)

INTRODUCING THE STORY

Stories about Coyote are among the most widely distributed Native American trickster tales, being found across the Great Plains, in the Southwest, and through California and Oregon. Sometimes the animal uses his wits to help others, but most often to fulfill his selfish desires. Not infrequently his plans backfire, with disastrous consequences to himself. Among the Zuni Pueblo people of western New Mexico, Coyote is generally presented as a self-centered, self-destructive fool. In a culture that celebrates balance and harmony, with individuals working together for the good of all, he is constantly trying to be something he is not in order to inflate his ego, with little regard for how his actions affect others.

McDermott, who first discovered this story while reading Frank Cushing's late-nineteenth-century collection of Zuni stories, develops it through a series of contrasts: coyote and the crows, the sky and land, the individual and the group, harmony and discord, and coyote at the beginning and the end. Coyote, who wishes to enhance his ego by flying like the birds, ends up falling to the ground and having his beautiful blue coat turned into a dirty gray. His failure results from his attempts to exceed his limitations and his refusal to work as a member

The crows circled Coyote but didn't carry him. Instead, they took back their feathers, one by one.

of the group. At the conclusion, Coyote is back on the ground where he belongs; however, there is no indication that he has learned from his experience.

The story, which would be told to emphasize the dangers of excessive ego and attempts to exceed the individual's limitations, is also a pourquoi story, explaining reasons for the way coyotes now look. When they saw actual coyotes, people would remember the story and the lessons it embodies.

THE AUTHOR DISCUSSES THE STORY

When I first began visiting Zuni Pueblo and conducting art programs for the children at the A'shiwi School, I became interested in the stories of Coyote. I read Cushing's versions and learned more from the children about the story. They explained that the birds were actually crows (who are very clever) and that they deliberately set out to cause Coyote to fall from the sky. The children also told me that after he'd fallen, Coyote chased the birds and tumbled into the water; that was when the gray dirt stuck to him, covering the blue.

Coyote, to me, is a kind of antihero. His adventure ends in disaster. I wanted to capture his annoying, abrasive character through color. Orange and blue clash when they are placed next to each other because they are complementary colors, opposites on the color spectrum. I limited the number of colors in the book, and these two embodied the tensions and conflicts in the story. Placing the blue against the orange background created a color clash that reflected the themes and character contrasts.

One of the real challenges that made working on this book different from creating the illustrations for *Zomo* and *Raven* was that I didn't have the lush backgrounds of the jungle or Northwest Coast forests. All the action of *Coyote* takes place in the thin air of the desert sky or on a mesa top. And so I set about to make the sky a "character" by using broad sweeping brushstrokes to suggest a very powerful presence. The orange backgrounds make Coyote and the crows stand out and create a luminosity.

I also drew on Pueblo art styles, particularly the repetition, with subtle variation, of basic design patterns. You can see this in Coyote's feathers and the dancing crows. At first glance they look the same, but there are small differences in each one. Old Man Crow wears a pendant that resembles Zuni coral, turquoise, jet, and shell jewelry. I was very pleased when the children at the school created a dramatic rendition of the story they'd helped me to tell.

Engagement Activities

Begin a **first reading** by having viewers carefully examine the front and back cover illustrations of the book, noticing all the differences. Among these are the size of the illustrations, the fact that the back illustration has a border, the color of coyote, his expression, and his body language. Make a list of these differences and explain to the children that these indicate changes that have occurred to Coyote during the story. After studying the list and the two illustrations, they can suggest what the changes might reveal about Coyote. Tell them that the story will explain why and how the changes come about.

Looking at the introductory material, pause to examine the triangular symbol on the dedication page. If the students know other McDermott books, they will be familiar with the author's use of symbols for important characters. Ask them to look for it in the pictures that follow and to see to whom it belongs. As they view and listen, children should look for contrasts and conflicts and for actions that may cause the changes indicated by the cover illustrations.

Read and show the pictures without comment. After the reading, return to the front and back illustrations, asking what caused the changes. This can lead into a discussion of the story conflicts. Students can discuss Coyote's interaction with the crows, why his actions are wrong, and how the crows resolve the conflict. In terms of Coyote's misbehaving and having a nose for mischief, how final is the resolution? Students can discuss what Coyote has learned, if anything, and whether they think he will ever reform. They can discuss both what Zuni children would have learned from the story and what they themselves have learned.

On a **second reading**, have the children look carefully at the illustrations, noticing Coyote's body language and facial expressions, along with those of the crows. They can discuss the different attitudes and character traits these reveal. Have them also notice how the illustrations present the conflicts between the individual and the group. They can notice that the birds are all in a balanced order, that they are frequently facing away from Coyote, and that their expressions reveal increasing annoyance with him. The way they are presented in each illustration can be contrasted to Coyote, whose position on the page, body language, and spatial relationship with the birds indicate his difference and their annoyance with him. In studying the various pictures, students can discuss the significance of the following phrases in the text as these relate to character, theme, and conflict: "out of step," "out of tune," "off balance."

Students can end their discussion of Coyote by considering his motives for wanting to fly. They should note that he is driven by ego, wanting to be "the greatest coyote in all the world." Why is Coyote's wanting to fly so foolish? He wants to be something he is not and for selfish reasons. If this is so, why do the birds agree to let him join them? They recognize his foolishness and want to have some fun with him. However, when he is boastful, rude, and demanding, exhibiting qualities frowned upon in the Zuni culture, the crows no longer want just to have fun. They become angry and decide to punish him by plucking his feathers.

On a **third reading**, students can focus directly on the illustrations of Coyote, looking carefully at his body language and facial expressions. Looking at each picture in sequence, noticing the context of the action, they can suggest adjectives that indicate Coyote's attitudes and personality in the specific situation. After all the pictures have been studied, students can examine the sequence of adjectives, looking to see if they can find a pattern in Coyote's changing attitudes and emotions, a pattern that indicates why his adventure ended the way it did, why he was responsible for its outcome. The adjectives can be entered in the "Dictionary of Character and Emotions." Words to describe the crows can also be entered.

Extension Activities

Literature: Read the two sentences on the last page that begin "To this day . . . " and discuss Coyote's physical appearance. Then have students discuss the appearances of actual coyotes. Explain that the Zuni story explained why and how coyotes first acquired their dusty color and black-tipped tail. Ask the children if they remember the term for a story explaining the original of natural or animal characteristics. *Coyote* is a pourquoi story, as are McDermott's *Raven, Papagayo, Jabutí the Tortoise, Anansi the Spider*, and *Daughter of Earth*. Unlike *Papagayo, the Mischief Maker*, which was an original McDermott story, this one is directly based on Zuni traditions and tales. Children can be invited to link *Coyote* to the other McDermott pourquoi stories. They might also like to read Rudyard Kipling's *Just So Stories*, original tales that provide fanciful explanations for animal characteristics.

Dancing, as a communal, culturally unifying activity, is an underlying theme of this story. Group unity is enhanced when members of the group work together in a dance that has significance to the entire society. McDermott explores this theme in both *Coyote* and *Arrow to the Sun*. Children can compare the situation of Coyote in relation to the dancing crows with the Boy and the dancing villagers in *Arrow to the Sun*, noticing how Coyote is an outsider in relation to the dancing crows, whereas the Boy has created unity and harmony among the dancing villagers to whom he is now a hero.

Coyote's foolish antics are not unlike those displayed by the trickster-fool in *Borreguita and the Coyote* (retold by Verna Aardema), *Ma'ii and Cousin Horned Toad* (retold by Shonto Begay), and *Coyote and the Magic Words* (retold by Phyllis Root). Children may wish to compare and contrast the characteristics of Coyote in these stories with those in McDermott's. Coyote's foolish antics can be compared to those of such other Native tricksters as Wesakajak (Cree), Nanabozho (Ojibwa), and Iktomi (Lakota).

Other Zuni stories the children may enjoy reading are Tony Hillerman's adaptation of the old Zuni folktale *The Boy Who Made Dragon Fly* and more tales about Coyote found in Frank Cushing's *Zuni Folktales.*

Language Arts: During the story, the following words are applied to Coyote: "winced," "twitched," "jerky," "tilted," "cringed," "struggled." Have the students create or look up definitions of these words and then explain why they are appropriate words for the story's "hero." It is interesting to notice that none of these words suggests balance or calmness; all of them relate to activities that are occasioned by Coyote's unsettling character and motivations.

At times, the characters' words in the story are accompanied by phrases like "he cried out" and "he demanded." Other times, the word "said" is used. Have the students find the places where "said" is used and have them replace that word with a more colorful word or phrase, one that is appropriate to the situation and the character's action.

Only Coyote and Old Man Crow speak during the story. However, in each scene in which they are present, the rest of the crows seem to be observing the action very carefully. Remind the students that although each of the "follower" crows looks the same at a first glance, each is subtly different. Each is an individual working harmoniously in the group. What might each of the crows be thinking about what is happening in each of the pictures? Brainstorm with the students, having them suggest different thoughts for each crow. Six children can suggest ideas for one picture; six for the next, and so forth. Then each child can draw a picture of a crow with a thought balloon above it. In the balloon, the student can write what the crow is thinking.

Only the head crow, Old Man Crow, has a symbol. Have the students discuss why the symbol is appropriate for the crow. They can then design a symbol for the crow for which they created "thoughts." After designing the symbol they can write a short paragraph explaining why it is appropriate for "their" crow.

Art: Have the students carefully study Coyote's face and ears, noticing how the artist changes details in order to indicate the character's different emotions. Basically, Coyote's face is a narrow, inverted triangle, with changes to eyes, ears, nose, and tongue. Write a list of emotional words that could apply to Coyote; then have the children draw a narrow, inverted triangle and create facial details to suggest one of the emotions. You could then read another Coyote tale from Cushing's collection and have the children illustrate it using the inverted triangle technique.

Social Studies and Science: Before writing *Coyote*, McDermott carefully researched traditional cultural elements of Zuni life so that he could better make the story reflect the values of the people who originally told it. After reading several Zuni stories, children can discuss how the characters' actions and attitudes in them reflect aspects of Zuni life, both behaviors that were approved and disapproved of. If they can find examples of traditional and modern Zuni art, they can try to see how McDermott incorporated these into his own art. They may wish to listen to Zuni music and find out the importance of different dances in Zuni culture. Children can also study how the Zuni people, especially children of their own age, live today.

The story also includes elements of the western New Mexico landscape, vegetation, and animal life. Have students make a list of the objects and animals in the story. They can then look up books on the natural life of the area to find out information about the area. They might also want to discuss what other living creatures are found in the area and then search collections of Pueblo folklore to see if there are stories about them.

Just as Coyote stories are distributed across large portions of North America, so too are the actual animals. In fact, they are found in wilderness, rural, suburban, and even urban areas. Students can study the habits of the coyote, researching in the library and online. They can also, where possible, report on their own observations about coyotes or can interview adults who have had encounters with the animals. After they have gathered their research, they might wish to consider why so many cultures have wanted to create coyote stories and how story coyotes and real coyotes are similar and different.

References

Aardema, Verna, reteller. Illustrated by Peter Mathers. *Borreguita and the Coyote.* New York: Alfred A. Knopf, 1991.

Begay, Shonto, reteller and illustrator. *Ma'ii and Cousin Horned Toad: A Traditional Navajo Story.* New York: Scholastic, 1992.

Cushing, Frank, collector. *Zuni Folktales.* Tucson: University of Arizona Press, 1988.

Hillerman, Tony, reteller. *The Boy Who Made Dragonfly.* Albuquerque, NM: University of New Mexico Press, 1972.

Kipling, Rudyard. *Just So Stories for Little Children.* London: Pan Books, 1975.

Root, Phyllis, reteller. Illustrated by Sandra Speidel. *Coyote and the Magic Words.* New York: Lothrop, Lee & Shepard, 1993.

MUSICIANS OF THE SUN

(1997)

INTRODUCING THE STORY

Like *Daughter of Earth* and *Raven*, which preceded it, and *Creation*, which followed, *Musicians of the Sun* recounts the transformation of a world of darkness and gloom into one suffused with light and color. Based on a Sixteenth-century document containing a fragment of Aztec mythology, the story came to McDermott's attention in the 1980s. He quickly outlined a version of the narrative text and sketched a small dummy delineating the actions and major figures. However, although these remained relatively unchanged in the book's final form, when McDermott returned to the project nearly a decade later, the finished art revealed that he had conceived new thematic dimensions of the story.

An outline of the plot indicates why the myth immediately "spoke to him, chose him," as he has said of the stories he has adapted. When Lord of the Night witnesses people laboring in a dark and joyless world, he directs Wind to free four musicians held captive by Sun and take them to the Earth. Armed with a shield, a thundercloud, and lightning, Wind makes the long journey, assisted across a vast sea by three female maritime helpers. He uses the weapons to take the musicians from their bondage and, in carrying them to Earth, brings light, color, music, and dance to the people.

Like many McDermott books, the story involves a long, dangerous quest in which the journeyer brings a boon to human beings. Specifically, it is associated with the sun, whose power is necessary for the story's agrarian people, and it involves a transformation of both the central character and the world to which he has a relationship. The conflicts of the story arise because initially there is no middle ground between opposing forces. The hero, in bringing the boon, mediates between two gods, Night and Sun, as their actions relate to two worlds: the heavens and earth. Although the achievement of success finally rests on the shoulders of the quester, he is aided by others.

In bringing the story to its final form, McDermott engaged in extensive research into traditional Aztec culture and incorporated relevant aspects into his visual and verbal narrative. The agricultural basis of Aztec life, the personification of forces of nature in Aztec gods, and the depiction of struggles between important gods in the traditional myths are all parts of McDermott's adaptation. His artwork similarly communicates Aztec concepts. This is apparent in the title page, which includes the idea of stars as eyes, the owl as a bird of night that

Now Sun was shining above the horizon.
Wind took a great breath and leaped into the sky.
As he flew up toward the house of the Sun
he heard the sweet music of flute, drum,
shell, and rattle.
"Musicians of the Sun," called Wind,
"I am coming to free you!"

symbolizes Lord of Night's nocturnal vision, and the circle, which reappears as the mirror that enables Lord to perceive the people's joyless existence and so to initiate Wind's quest. These images communicate the themes of darkness and enlightenment that inform the narrative.

Ideas of insight and enlightenment are central, as well, to the non-culture-specific themes of the story. McDermott has spoken of this myth as paralleling the journey the imagination makes in bringing light and form to the sometimes chaotic fragments of darkness and of articulating them as unified artistic creations. The opposite poles of this movement to creation are characterized by McDermott's choice of color for the endpapers—the blue at the front relating to the world of night and the red at the back symbolizing the warmth and light now experienced on Earth. The concept of growing perception is articulated through changes depicted on the face of the mirror. The increasing clarity and detail of the images relate to the formative stages of artistic concepts. However, the grayness and dreariness of the world depicted can be transformed only by bringing a full spectrum of color, a rainbow of life and harmony that is embodied in the four differently colored musicians. As their color and, by extension, the harmonious vitality of their music infuse the world, the people are revitalized, reenergized in their life-sustaining work. Such is the effect of the end product of artistic creation—the revitalizing effect of this harmonious articulation of what had been fragments of the imagination.

THE AUTHOR DISCUSSES THE STORY

I tried to create a work that is a reflection of my emotional and intellectual responses to life and to combine these with the essence of the original story. I was attracted to the idea of the journey and the coming back with a boon that would bring life to a wasteland. I felt that the story reflected the journey of the artist who opened the way for young minds to come to fuller imaginative lives. At the end of *Musicians of the Sun*, you see a much richer world, a truly revitalized land. I think myths can perform a parallel function for children. To do this, I had to allow ideas and emotions to emerge from my unconscious and take form, to become a kind of light.

I sketched out the story in words and images very early on, and that outline didn't change a great deal. But over a decade, I think the meaning of the myth was beginning to assume a form that I may not have been aware of. Just like Wind coming from the darkness to light, so too did the completed retelling. One of the things that happened was that during the time the myth was gestating, I was developing greater control over my art. What emerged was a story closer to my internal vision of it. The final visual element of the myth, with its use of less color or more color, contrasted the relatively straightforward verbal narrative with the underlying sense of spiritual mystery and power.

One of the challenges was to convey visually the significance of the music, the revitalizing forces Wind liberated and brought to human beings. The colors in the later pages became the visual equivalent of sound. I tried to make the pages musical through my use of color, to create a visual parallel between the coming of music and an infusion of color. I tried to create a sense of musical harmonies and the progression of musical notes. Linking the two and showing the figures almost dancing to the music they're playing helped to communicate the idea of the arts as an organic whole and part of a unified, complete life.

When I set out to do the final art work, I looked at several kinds of hand-made paper. The type I chose, appropriately, was made in Mexico and contained cactus fiber. Its texture suggested ancient manuscript materials, and I was able to play off the colors against the background texture. In a way, the colors seemed to emerge out of darkness, which paralleled the plot and theme.

Engagement Activities

Before a **first reading**, write the word "transformation" on the board and have the student's discuss the term's meaning, along with any ideas about change that it might suggest to them. Then, without indicating a link, introduce the book, showing first the cover, then the front and back endpapers. Ask what the students notice about the endpapers: the change in colors. What word does the change suggest? Transformation. Explain that the story will deal with the idea of transformation or change. As they listen to the words and view the illustrations, they should be searching for transformations.

After the reading, return to the colored endpapers, inviting the students to offer suggestions about why McDermott might have chosen these two colors. This discussion can provide a lead in to a consideration of the story's visual and thematic transformations. In visual terms, the students can notice the movement from a world of night, to one of brilliant sun, to one in which a full spectrum of color exists. The human world is depicted first in gray and later in a variety of colors; the people's body language changes, as does that of the musicians. During the course of his travels, Wind acquires more and more color. Other transformations include the status of the lives of the people and the musicians, as well as the emotions of Sun.

Before a **second reading**, suggest to the students that the visual and intangible transformations occur because of the resolution of conflicts. Ask them what they think the major conflict of the story is, the one that is introduced near the beginning and not resolved until near the end. The joyless life of the people is not altered until Wind brings the musicians from the Sun. Explain that before this primary conflict is resolved, there are many secondary ones that must be successfully encountered if Wind is going to continue his quest to its conclusion. They should look for these conflicts and notice the means of their resolution. Among these are Wind's fear of the journey and Lord of the Night's providing him protection and weapons; the impossibility of crossing the sea alone and the help of the three females; the attack by Sun and Wind's use of the shield; the darkness of the journey to Earth and his use of the lightning. Students may wish to discuss the reasons why Wind must overcome these various difficulties before he is able to succeed in his quest to bring the musicians to Earth.

A **third reading** can focus on the role of the illustrations in communicating the conflicts and themes. Students can be reminded of the importance of the different colored endpapers. Read aloud the text of the four opening double-spreads, noting afterward that there are only eighty-one words. Invite students to look at the four pictures, along with the title, copyright, and dedication pages. What is added from page to page, and how might the additions be important to the themes and conflict? Notice that to the owl and mirror of the title page are added a number of objects that come together to form Lord of the Night. The circle on the title page becomes Lord's mirror, which contains an increasingly more detailed picture, one that explains the nature of the story's main problem. The idea of viewers being able to see more clearly Lord of Night and the objects in the mirror foreshadows the light that later enables the human world to be seen in full color and the people to end their sadness.

Students can also notice that as he overcomes the obstacles encountered on the quest, Wind acquires more color. At first he has only a red beak, later some turquoise, then green, and then orange as he moves to the Sun. The colors spread to different parts of his body. It's as if he is becoming fuller, more complex as a result of the beings he encounters on his travels.

In a concluding discussion, point out to students that a rainbow links the musicians and Wind. Ask them why the colored rainbow should link the four colored musicians to the now more colorful Wind. How has the interaction between musicians and Wind been beneficial to both? Have the students note that the newly liberated musicians represent a harmony of color, sound, and dance that brings light and renewed life to the land, and joy to the people. Ask what we call people who create harmonious music, dance, and visual art. They are artistic creators. Who is instrumental in the creation of these harmonies in this story? Wind is an artist, a creator, who becomes more fulfilled as an individual when his work brings joy and enrichment to the people.

Extension Activities

Literature: This work is as rich in links to McDermott's other books as any of his stories are. For example, as a questing hero, Wind is similar to the Boy (*Arrow to the Sun*) and Yvain (*Knight of the Lion*). The people's joy at being released from a world of dreariness is also seen in *Raven*, and *Daughter of Earth*. A journey into the sky is found in *Sunflight, Daniel O'Rourke, Raven, Coyote, Arrow to the Sun*, and *Jabutí the Tortoise*. Dance plays a role in *Arrow to the Sun* and *Daniel O'Rourke*. And, of course, many characters, including the Boy, Tasaku (*The Stonecutter*), Osiris (*The Voyage of Osiris*), and Coyote undergo transformations—not all of them positive—as a result of their experiences. Using the "Family of Stories" chart, students can find as many links and visual similarities between *Musicians of the Sun* and McDermott's other stories. They should be encouraged to notice not only similarities but also differences between the stories. They can be reminded that each story is unique and is a reflection of the distinct culture that originated it.

Deborah Nourse Lattimore's *The Flame of Peace: A Tale of the Aztecs* and David Wisniewski's *Rain Player*, which draws on ancient Mayan culture, offer interesting comparisons to *Musicians of the Sun* in their use of Central American mythology. Lattimore employs highly stylized art resembling the art of the ancient Aztecs to tell the story of Two Flint, who makes a dangerous quest to the land of Lord Morning Star in search of peace for his people. Her depictions of Wind, as well as the quest journey, can be compared to those in *Musicians*. Wisniewski uses cut paper in his account of a boy who engages in a life-and-death struggle to bring rain to his people. The violence and conflict in the stories and the resolutions achieved can be compared to those in *Musicians*.

Language Arts: In many ways, this book is about seeing, perceiving. In the early pictures the images become progressively clearer; as the story advances, increasingly brighter colors make the settings more distinct. Of course, McDermott uses his illustrations to communicate this theme; the verbal text is very spare. Students might wish to have others who have not encountered the book "see" it through language. They can create description, narration, dialogue, and even accounts of characters' thoughts. One organizational principle might be to write McDermott's text for each double-spread and then write about setting and events, moving from left to right as the action does in the first two-thirds of the book and, later, from right to left. Beginning with the title page, the owl appears in seven consecutive illustrations. It is again seen in the final double-spread. In all of them, it appears to be looking directly toward the viewer. Have students pretend that they are having a conversation with the owl. Working in pairs, one student can direct questions to the bird about his reactions to what is happening and the other can supply answers.

Students who are keeping a "Dictionary of Character and Emotions" can select words for Lord of the Night, Wind, and Sun.

Social Studies: Like the Pueblo culture depicted in *Arrow to the Sun* and that of the ancient Greeks in *Daughter of Earth*, the Aztec civilization was agrarian. Students may wish to compare these three societies and suggest how the three myths McDermott has retold reflect the cultures' beliefs and attitudes. How do the stories reflect traits shared by agricultural societies and how, when compared, does each reveal distinct characteristics? After looking at the images of the farm laborers in Lord of the Night's mirror, students can study the agricultural practices of the Aztecs. What were the main crops? How were they planted, cultivated, and harvested? What class of people performed the labor? What were the conditions of their lives? Students may wish to examine the other major element of Aztec society, its warrior culture, and suggest how *Musicians of the Sun* reflects elements of it.

The Arts: If some students have written expanded texts for the myth, other students unfamiliar with McDermott's adaptation can study the artistic style of Aztec Mexico, noting the symbolic significances of various objects and beings; the clothing, hair styles, and ornaments of people of various ranks and classes; and architecture. The results of these studies can be incorporated into their own illustrations.

In classes where this writing and illustration project is not being undertaken, students can study the same materials and note where McDermott has used Aztec art in his illustrations, how he has modified it, and how it is used to impart meaning to the story he tells.

In addition to the arrival of Lord of Night into the universe and Wind's travels to the Sun and then to Earth, movement is significant to two groups in the story: the musicians and the laborers. Each group is seen in contrasting situations. Tied to the Sun, the four musicians are constricted in their movements; liberated, they dance as they play. The farm laborers in the grey world appear to be cultivating in a repetitive, lock-step fashion; when light, color, and music arrive, they cast aside their implements, join hands, and dance. Students can divide into groups and engage in movement that reflects both the before and after activities of the two groups and their movements as they become aware of the changes taking place in their lives.

References

Lattimore, Deborah Nourse. *The Flame of Peace: A Tale of the Aztecs.* New York: Harper and Row, 1987.

Wisniewski, David. *Rain Player.* New York: Clarion Books, 1991.

JABUTÍ THE TORTOISE:
A TRICKSTER TALE FROM THE AMAZON

(2001)

INTRODUCING THE STORY

Like many tricksters, the title hero of *Jabutí the Tortoise* (whose name is pronounced zha-boo-CHEE) must use his wits to succeed in a world where the other animals are larger, stronger, and swifter than he is. And, like other tricksters, he is sometimes beneficent, employing his cleverness to help others, and frequently selfish. He is occasionally outwitted by other creatures. McDermott draws on each of these elements to tell the Amazonian version of a tale-type found in many parts of the world: the story of how the tortoise (or turtle) acquired its cracked shell. He also places emphasis on a theme that has been important in many of his later works, the idea that creation—embodied in his stories as music and color—comes from chaos. Color and music give light and joy to a world of darkness.

As was the case in the other books in McDermott's trickster series, the written narrative begins and ends with very simple sentences. The tortoise is described playing his flute, with the music flowing through and rising above the jungle. There are significant differences between beginning and end. On the opening page appears the sentence: "His shell was smooth and shiny and his

They had almost reached heaven when Vulture suddenly swooped and turned upside down.

Jabuti lost hold of Vulture's feathers and slipped off his back.

song was sweet." This is modified on the final page to read: "His shell may be cracked and patched, but his song is sweet . . . at least to some." His appearance has changed, but the song remains sweet. The earlier sentence is in the past tense, the later one in the present. Things are now different from what they once were, and the intervening visual and verbal narrative explains how and why the change has occurred.

Of course, the changes are the results of a conflict in which Jabutí has become involved. He had earlier used his musical abilities to trick Jaguar, Lizard, Tapir, and Whale into performing acts that either amused him or were beneficial only to him. However, the birds "loved Jabutí's song" and sang along. At this point, the first of the two major conflicts is introduced. Vulture is jealous of the tortoise's musical ability and his popularity with the birds. When the land-bound tortoise is unable to join a festival in heaven, Vulture uses deceit to cause Jabutí to shatter his shell, exposing the meal the scavenger desires. The other birds' restore their friend's fragmented shell and receive their distinctive bright colors as a reward for their actions. Vulture remains black and tuneless. The restored trickster continues his music and mischief to this day.

Although the story reflects McDermott's statement about the emergence of creativity from chaos, it also reveals the ambiguity of the central character and raises many implicit questions. Has Jabutí been using his musical talents wisely? Is he—a land animal—exceeding his limitations by wanting to ascend with the birds? Would Vulture have sought revenge had the tortoise always been altruistic in his actions? Has his fall led Jabutí to alter his negative ways?

The illustrations reveal Jabutí's changing position in his world. In the opening double-spread he is balanced on one side of the page, with flowers and butterflies and birds on the other; however, in the pictures that include Vulture, he is much smaller and lower on the page. Only at the end is the situation reversed. Jabutí dominates the page, with his bird friends flying above him. Defeated Vulture is behind him and much smaller. It is interesting to note that the pictures of the jungle world that reflect the brilliant colors of the environment are painted with a glossy texture that sets them off from the flat colors of the sky world. Jabutí's natural environment is the land, not the sky. He is out of place above the ground.

THE AUTHOR DISCUSSES THE STORY

I'd read a large number of South American tales years ago and had been particularly interested in the trickster Jabutí—that's the name of a small South American land tortoise. I liked the sense of compassion in the stories. I realized that this tale was more than just a pourquoi tale about why the tortoise's is cracked. It's a story about friendship and betrayal, compassion, death and rebirth. I saw the story as a metaphor for ideas about healing and joining together.

When I began my research for the story, finding out about cultural and artistic aspects of the lives of the people from the Amazonian rainforests, I didn't discover any visual representations of Jabutí. I was pleased about that, because it released me to create my own designs to picture the hero in a way that was unique to this story. I began doing a series of pencil sketches, working to find an image that reflected his personality—his insouciance. In this tale, he's a victim; the trickster is tricked. But he is a mischief-maker, like the other tricksters. I depicted some of his earlier adventures when he used his wits to overcome bigger, stronger, faster animals. He was having fun at their expense. The flute he plays in this book was made from the thigh bone of a jaguar he'd tricked in an earlier story.

One of the things I noticed while I was researching the South American backgrounds was that nearly every book about the Amazon that I picked up—anthropology, biology, folktales—seemed to have a green cover. So I decided to do something different, something people wouldn't expect. I became a kind of trickster. Green wouldn't be my dominant background color—I used a hot Brazilian pink.

Engagement Activities

As with the presentation of the other trickster stories, discussion of this one can begin with an examination of the front and back covers. Students can note that Jabutí's shell has changed and, if they already know the term *pourquoi story*, can predict what this story will explain. They should also be encouraged to notice the flute and suggest how it might be significant. They might wish to examine carefully the ways Jabutí's "fingers" are holding the flute. He seems to be playing different notes in the two pictures. How might that be important?

As you begin a **first reading**, ask listeners and viewers to interrupt when they sense the beginning of a conflict. The first major conflict starts when Vulture is introduced. Remind readers that a story can have more than one conflict. Some conflicts they might notice include Jabutí's inability to get to the festival, Vulture's throwing him off his back, the shattering of the shell, and the King of Heaven's shaming of Vulture. After finishing the first reading, students should reexamine their interpretations of the front and back covers, modifying and expanding them as appropriate. They can also look at the colors of the endpapers, the design of the title page, and the symbol on the dedication page, relating these to the visual and verbal narrative that follows. The title page is particularly interesting, containing as it does the colors of the river, land, and sky and, in the four corners, the fragments of tortoise's once-smooth shell.

Before a **second reading**, review the list of conflicts the students noticed during the first reading. Introduce the term *resolution* and ask the students to notice which of these conflicts are resolved and how. In discussing the resolutions, one focus can be on how the conflicts arise from bad relationships between characters and are resolved through cooperation among others. Students can notice that Vulture's selfish jealousy is punished with a reprimand and that the other birds' assistance is rewarded with new colors.

Before concluding a discussion of conflict and resolutions, read the parallel opening and closing lines. Then ask the students if there are any unresolved conflicts. They may discuss Vulture's unfulfilled desire for revenge. Should they do so, they might wish to look at the final picture for details suggesting that the conflict between Vulture and Jabutí might continue beyond the story. Finally, students can remember that Jabutí played tricks on other land creatures. Do they think that he has been cured of this habit?

A **third reading** can focus directly on the illustrations as they reveal Jabutí's attitudes, the developing conflict, and the nature of the relationships between the various characters. They can notice the size of Jabutí and his placement in each picture. For example, in the opening picture, he fits harmoniously into the landscape and does not dominate the page. His relationship with the birds shows the smaller colored birds on the same side of the page, with all of them flying toward him. Vulture is on the opposite side, looming ominously; his feathers are black and gray. He becomes progressively larger than the tortoise as he dominates the conflict. On the second to last illustration, Jabutí dances and plays happily, balanced by his avian benefactors. Only Vulture's head is seen as it juts from the edge of the picture. He has lost the struggle. However, he is still around, and as his facial expression reveals, he is still angry. Students can enter appropriate words for Jabutí and Vulture in their "Dictionary of Character and Emotions."

Extension Activities

Literature: *Jabutí the Tortoise* invites comparison with two other McDermott stories involving disastrous sky-flights: *Sunflight* and *Coyote*. Students can compare the nature of the three unsuccessful flights and discuss the reasons for their failures. Both Coyote and Icarus are responsible for what happens to them. Although both Coyote and Jabutí are "let down" by birds and as a result acquire distinguishing physical characteristics, Coyote deserves to be dropped by birds to whom he behaves rudely. Jabutí, a friend of some birds, experiences what is, in a way, a "fortunate fall" because the colors of his shell are transferred to his rescuers. In both stories, the pourquoi elements link the natural world to the lessons of the story. Seeing the tortoise's shell, the birds' bright colors, or Coyote's burnt tail, people are reminded of the character virtues and weaknesses that, according to the stories, led to the acquisition of these distinctive markings.

As the author's introductory note indicates, many of the stories about Jabutí may have developed from West African trickster tales that were brought to the Americas with the enslaved Africans. There are, indeed, many similarities between the Amazonian Tortoise stories, North American Brer Rabbit stories, and West African Tortoise and Rabbit tales. "Tug-of-War" in Julius Lester's *How Many Spots Does a Leopard Have?* is a version of an event briefly alluded to in *Jabutí the Tortoise.* In "Brer Rabbit Finally Gets Beaten," from Lester's *The Tales of Uncle Remus*, Brer Turtle outwits the trickster. In Tololwa Mollel's *Ananse's Feast: An Ashanti Tale*, the well-known trickster is outwitted by a turtle. Students can compare the tales.

Language Arts: Like many of McDermott's stories, *Jabutí the Tortoise* is organized around a series of contrasts or oppositions. A discussion of these could lead to a consideration of antonyms, pairs of words that mean the opposite of each other. Among those in this story are sky–earth, loyalty–betrayal, whole–fragmented. Students should try to find as many paired opposites (both explicit and implicit) as they can in the story and then discuss these as they relate to conflicts and their resolutions.

In two illustrations, a fish observes the characters and events. It has no part in the story itself, but seems to be a kind of silent commentator. Students can write a paragraph from the fish's point of view. This paragraph can contain both an account of what's happening and the fish's thoughts about the events. The river is seen in two other illustrations, although the fish isn't. Students could assume that it is still observing and thinking and could write paragraphs for these pages as well.

Students who enjoy creative writing may wish to write versions of Jabutí's successful trickster episodes alluded to early in the story. A good starter would be to have students read versions of the tug-of-war tale involving other animals and then transpose events to the tortoise. Writing stories for the other two episodes, students might wish to use the following questions: Why did Jabutí want to perform this particular trick? What were the victims like—clever, foolish, vain, or something else? How did Jabutí proceed to make the trick work?

Social Studies and Science: Understanding and enjoyment of the story can be enhanced when the students engage in background research. Although McDermott's birds are somewhat generic, students can ask what kinds of actual South American birds might have wanted to help Jabutí. They could find out about their appearances and activities. What kind of Vulture might have carried Jabutí? How big would he have been in comparison to the type of tortoise (Jabutí) that the hero is supposed to be? In the picture in which Vulture takes Jabutí into the sky, the river appears to be clean and is surrounded by jungle. In the early twenty-first century, would this still be the case? Students can discuss the problems of deforestation and the attendant river pollution. How might these ecological disasters be affecting the types of birds, animals, and fish found in the area? Is the Jabutí tortoise an endangered species?

Although this McDermott story contains very few visual or verbal cultural references, it is nonetheless a story that reflects the values of traditional rainforest people. Students can examine the beliefs of the aboriginal peoples of this area, especially their attitudes toward specific birds and animals, particularly vultures and tortoises. What qualities or values did these creatures represent or embody? What role did storytelling play in the people's lives, and what, specifically, were the purposes of telling Jabutí tales?

Students who have studied African, African American, and Caribbean trickster stories might wish to consider how many of these stories could have been brought to the New World on the slave ships. They can trace the main slave routes from Africa to parts of the Western Hemisphere and then discuss how and why stories may have changed when they were told in specific countries.

The Arts: As noted, McDermott created his own stylized rainforest landscape rather than draw on traditional art styles of the Amazon. Students who have studied his use of appropriate styles in other works and who have written texts for the other Jabutí trickster stories might wish to research art, design, and clothing patterns of the area and then illustrate their stories using these as guides.

Students can listen to recordings of traditional Brazilian flute music, deciding which pieces they would use if they were to provide background music for a dramatization or film of the story.

References

Lester, Julius, reteller. Illustrated by David Shannon. *How Many Spots Does a Leopard Have? and Other Tales.* New York: Scholastic, 1989.

Lester, Julius, reteller. Illustrated by Jerry Pinkney. *The Tales of Uncle Remus: The Adventures of Brer Rabbit.* New York: Dial Books, 1987.

Mollel, Tololwa, M., reteller. Illustrated by Andrew Glass. *Ananse's Feast: An Ashanti Tale.* New York: Clarion Books, 1997.

CREATION

(2003)

INTRODUCING THE STORY

Creation is Gerald McDermott's most ambitious picture book, dealing as it does with one of the world's best-known stories, the biblical account of creation. On a first reading, its differences from the author's other works become quickly apparent. However, on further examination, it seems to share thematic and artistic similarities with the traditional stories he had earlier adapted.

Although there is a central character who initiates the action, he is not involved in any conflicts as are the heroes of the other tales. Indeed, the story is not structured on a movement from conflict to resolution; its movement is from darkness to light to full color, from a void to a universe filled with heavenly bodies, one of which, Earth, is abundant with vegetation and animal life. The first-person narrator, the first in McDermott's works, performs the acts of creation without opposition and with no apparent difficulty. He is never seen, and only the results of his work, not the actions themselves, are depicted. Moreover, there are no other characters who play roles in advancing the story.

Darkness, mist, water, light.
Seed, root, flower, tree,
and fruit.

However, the narrative presents the original and most majestic acts of creation and transformation, both actions and themes dealt with on human levels in *Arrow to the Sun* and *The Knight of the Lion* and cosmic levels in *Raven* and *Musicians of the Sun*. As in other works, color is one of the major vehicles for communicating the transformations. And, as with all of McDermott's books, the elements of creation and transformation of the outer world are seen as reflections of the process of self-creation and transformation within individuals. For all people, there is a beginning and an ongoing process of creation, which is also transformation.

Both in words and pictures, McDermott links the macrocosmic transformation recounted in Genesis, Chapter 1, and the microcosmic creation of the individual in and later beyond the womb. The narrator speaks in a rhythmic prose,

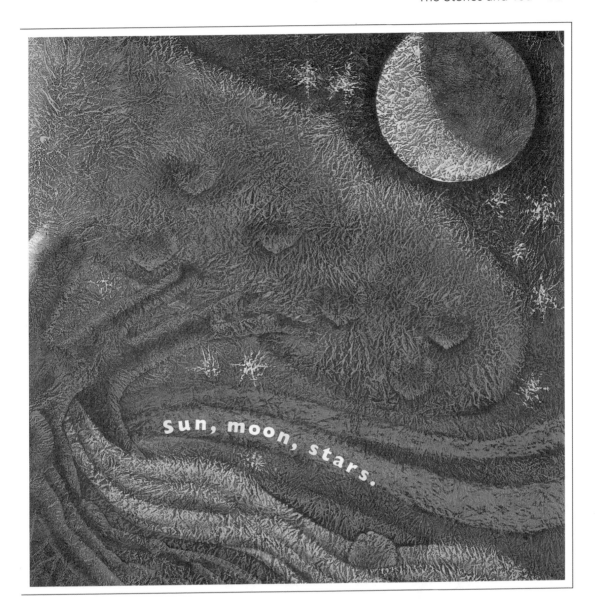

reporting on what he created out of darkness. As the God of the Hebrew Bible existed in a world of darkness and through His words spoke light into being and separated the waters surrounding him, so individuals, alone in the womb, are aware of only themselves as they exist in the darkness and water. Individuals, like the biblical creator, fashion their own realities through perception and articulation. The heavenly bodies, vegetation, and animals exist for individuals because these are seen. The final illustration of a fetus and the circular sentences "I am all this. All this I AM" implicitly link cosmic and individual creation. The birth of each child is a reenactment, a renewal of the original creation.

The illustrations also link the narrative to the creative work of the artist. Ideas are initially the artist's alone, existing in the depths of the unconscious.

Gradually they take shape and form and become visible. They are, as it were, brought to life. They are given color and acquire a vitality that extends beyond the vehicle (film, book, painting) through which they are expressed. As depicted, the light, the sun, and the created beings seem to move beyond the pages of *Creation*. The work of art is a vehicle, the life of which goes into the world. If it is successful, it assumes new life in the readers, viewers, and listeners, who repeat the act of creation initiated by the artist. The creative force is ALL, being constantly reborn.

It should also be noted that, through the illustrations, McDermott links the mythological, personal, and artistic to scientific ideas. The early illustrations of the coming of light and the spirals of the animals circling and moving toward the earth suggest nebula, from the swirling of which new worlds and galaxies may be created, and DNA spirals, which contain the essences out of which life is created.

McDermott has stated that he wanted to make his version of the creation story both non-sectarian and personal, so that individuals of all beliefs could respond to the majesty, the miracle of the creations of the world around them and themselves. By using an unseen, unnamed narrator as the central character, by linking the great and the small, and by paralleling the scientific and the mythological, he has succeeded.

THE AUTHOR DISCUSSES THE STORY

This was a story I'd wanted to tell for over thirty years, but I didn't want to render it in narrowly religious terms. Instead I approached it with the sense of human connectedness that I found in all traditions. But it took all that time of immersing myself in stories from around the world before I was able to see the creation story as a metaphor for the birth of consciousness. I thought about what it would be like in the womb, floating in darkness, in a space where you are the be-all and end-all of existence, where you are outside of time. I heard a voice—mine—saying, "I was before time." That was the catalyst for the rest of the words. That's why I used the first person; creation isn't from outside; it begins as a spark inside. We create the world; it's what we perceive it to be. Our own world expands as our consciousness does.

The whole experience of the book—writing and illustrating it—was very liberating and fulfilling. It was extremely satisfying to roll ahead in an outwardly expanding spiral. I started from the small white dot—a point of light—expanding into light and then color. The book moves from an amorphous shadow world into a grand, majestic world of color, of being. In my use of color, *Raven* and *Musicians of the Sun* were preparations for this book. I had to hone my craft before I was able to deal with creation. When I came to *Creation*, I think I had acquired the skill I needed to show the transformation from darkness to light in a more powerful and organic way.

In creating the illustrations, I was influenced by William Blake, the Eighteenth-century English poet and painter; not by his specific style, but by his having created a highly personalized vision of his subject. His sketch of the Leviathan struck me; the spirit of that picture resonated when I did the animals of the hunt thundering across the page. So, I wanted the pictures to be personal, to embody my own vision of what creation was. I didn't want to give it the standard iconographic treatment.

Both the type of paper and the typography were important in communicating the dignity and majesty of the theme. A few years ago, when I was visiting a little village in Japan that is famous for its papermaking, I found paper created from crushed mulberry bark. Its texture helped to create the ancient quality I was seeking. The paper wouldn't allow the depiction of precise images. It resisted me. I had to be more painterly, using brush strokes to layer textures. It was very enjoyable to work with this paper. Some of the small faces, especially the gorilla, were accidentally formed by the interaction between the brush and the paper surface.

Joy Chu, a superb typographic designer, worked with me on the lettering of the text. We wanted a font choice and layout to parallel the spirit of the illustrations. There aren't blocks of text the way there are in most of my books. Words and pictures form an organic whole. The layout captures the rhythm of the sentences and parallels the visual aspects of the page.

Engagement Activities

Because this book deals more with concepts than with conflict and character development, discussion of the title word, "creation," should precede a **first reading**. Students in the upper elementary grades should be encouraged to explore both denotations and connotations of the word, including scientific, biological, artistic, and specifically religious meanings. The ideas should be listed so that, after the initial reading of the book, students can discuss how these are related to the subject matter and meanings of the book. Although the word is not used in the text, the concept of "transformation" is also significant to the theme. Students can also discuss this word and then consider how it might be linked to the term "creation."

The preliminary material should be carefully examined, with viewers noticing visual elements that could be significant in the pages to follow. Items important to consider are the spirals of animals, Earth, and the human beings on the title page, the shift from dark blue to forest green on the endpapers, the blackness of the title and copyright pages, and the small gray dot on the first page.

Read the story through slowly, allowing viewers plenty of time to study each double-spread illustration. After the reading, return to the preliminary pages and ask the students to link the details they noticed before reading the book to specific elements of the visual and verbal narrative. Then, they can reconsider the terms "creation" and "transformation," discussing ways they are important thematically to the narrative.

A **second reading** can consider the book in stages. The first part includes the gray dot and the statement about the narrator's existence. The second starts with the creation of night and day and ends with the creation of the first man and woman. The third is a recapitulation of the creation, while the fourth restates the creator's existence and presents a small dot surrounded by blackness—but with a difference. The focus should be on the illustrations and how they communicate not only the observable stages of creation but also the ideas and emotions connected with this magnificent process. Why are the images progressively more distinct? Why is more color included? How does the placement of the words reinforce the feelings evoked by the visuals? Students can notice that visually and verbally, the last two double-spreads recapture the stages of creation. Finally, they might consider why there is a fetus in the closing circle. Does the creation of a human being duplicate on a small scale the grand mystery of the original creation?

A **third reading** can focus on the text. Tell students that McDermott used only 224 words to narrate the account of a powerful, majestic event. Half of these words are nouns and verbs. Directional prepositions account for another 10 percent. As they listen, students can keep a list of the nouns, verbs, and adjectives (or the presenter could prepare a list on a transparency). After the reading, discuss the verbs, noting that some describe actions and others, states of being. Which of these verbs do students feel are particularly effective in depicting the acts of creation? Notice that the nouns move from references to intangible and indistinct things to more concrete, specific ones. The final nouns in the sequence of creation are man and woman. Students should note the words applied to their role in creation: "keepers" and "to care for." Discuss the idea of responsibility to the rest of creation. Notice also that the majority of the prepositions are directional; they imply movement from one place or state to another or change. Discuss how these types of prepositions are appropriate to a book about creation. Finally, students can compare the text of the opening and closing pages, discussing possible reasons for the shift from past to present and for the inverted order of the words of the last two sentences.

Extension Activities

Literature: Like *Raven* and *Musicians of the Sun, Creation* deals with a movement from darkness and indistinct images to light, color, and distinctness. McDermott has related the events of the three stories to the act of artistic creation. Students can be asked to notice the similarities among the three books and, after being told of the author-illustrator's having drawn parallels between the acts of the central characters and those of an artist, can discuss the artistic process, including their own work, as McDermott has described it.

Although McDermott avoids specific religious references in his retelling, the narrative draws on Chapter 1 of Genesis. Students can compare this "Western" creation myth with myths from other parts of the world. *In the Night, Still Dark*, by Richard Lewis, is an adaptation of a Hawaiian creation chant. Like *Creation*, it involves a movement from darkness to light, night to day, and concludes the sequence of creative acts with the formation of human beings. Paul Goble's *Remaking the Earth* is a Northern Plains version of a widely distributed Native American myth. A small bird dives to the depth of the waters that flood the earth and brings back a clump of mud that becomes the basis of land. Human beings are not the last created beings, as Earth Maker fashions horses to help the people. Virginia Hamilton's *In the Beginning* retells twenty-four creation tales from a wide variety of traditional cultures.

Language Arts: McDermott uses two interesting writing techniques to communicate the tones of his narrative. Students can study the use of parallel sentences in which the order of words and specific words are repeated to create a measured rhythm that enhances the grandness of the sequential acts of creation. He also uses a sequence of nouns, the names of the objects and beings, to suggest the fullness, the richness of creation. Having studied how these techniques are used, students can create their own parallel sentences to give the sense of a process like the approach and then presence of a storm or the arriving of spring. The festivities and foods of Thanksgiving can be listed in a way that indicates abundance, plenitude.

Social Studies and Science: Being nonsectarian, the book does not embody the art styles or values of specific cultures. The created beings appear to have come from all over (and under) the planet. Students could identify the animals depicted in the spirals and suggest where they might be found in the greatest abundance. They could then discuss what cultural significances the creatures hold for the people who live in the areas they inhabit. Students can then make a list of creatures found in their own environments and could create four spirals depicting them.

The man and woman were given the responsibility to care for the other created beings. To what extent have their descendents living in the region of the readers failed in their responsibilities? What are some of the extinct and endangered species, and how are the failures of human beings to exercise their caring duties responsible for these creatures' status?

The Arts: Visual interpretations of the Genesis creation story are found throughout the history of Western art. McDermott has discussed the grand conceptions of Michelangelo and the personal vision of William Blake. Students can study the works of these and other artists, discussing the emotional tones of the events depicted and how these are communicated.

The interplay between the textures of different types of paper and the various media of McDermott's books, particularly *Creation*, is an important element of creating the meanings and tones of his illustrations. Students might wish to experiment, as McDermott has, with different paper-media combinations, noticing the effects these produce. They could then choose one of these combinations to illustrate a scene from a creation myth of their choice.

References

Goble, Paul, reteller and illustrator. *Remaking the Earth: A Creation Story from the Great Plains of North America.* New York: Orchard Books, 1996.

Hamilton, Virginia, reteller. Illustrated by Barry Moser. *In the Beginning: Creation Stories from Around the World.* San Diego: Harcourt Brace Jovanovich, 1988.

Lewis, Richard. Illustrated by Ed Young. *In the Night, Still Dark.* New York: Atheneum, 1988.

Other McDermott Books Briefly Considered

THE MAGIC TREE
A TALE FROM THE CONGO
(1973)

A story from the Bakongo tribe of central Africa, *The Magic Tree* recounts a failed coming-of-age quest. The less favored of two twins, Mavungu leaves his childhood home, and after he has liberated a mythological princess from a tree, he is transformed. His new appearance reflects the revitalizing, ennobling powers of the woman. However, because he cannot break the ties to his childhood and because he betrays his wife, the young man loses everything. McDermott has commented on the importance of color in this story: "It was the first instance in which I worked with the color spectrum as an emotional spectrum. I wanted to contrast somber emotional moods with exciting ones. The hero fails to transform himself, to become an adult, because he makes the wrong choice between his mother and his wife. He fails to take advice from the wise and powerful woman who had given his life new dimensions."

Students in the middle and upper elementary grades can compare the earlier and later illustrations depicting Mavungu's transformations, discussing what the differences in details reveal about the reasons for and psychological nature of the changes. This can lead to a discussion of the causes of the failure of the quest. Viewers can also compare the colors in parallel scenes throughout the book and can relate these to theme, conflict, and character development. They can also create written texts for the wordless pages, particularly the last four. The art style of the book can be related to the low-relief carvings from the Congo and to the carved masks, many of which were used in male initiation stories.

THE VOYAGE OF OSIRIS
A MYTH OF ANCIENT EGYPT
(1977)

The first of his books that was neither preceded by or created along with a film, *The Voyage of Osiris* is one of the most widely known myths that McDermott has retold. It is also the second of the author's works to focus directly on what he has termed "the life-giving powers of women." When the god Osiris is imprisoned by his evil brother Set, his body is found by his wife and coruler, Isis. Later, Set dismembers Osiris's body, and it is Isis who must gather the parts, binding them together to give her husband new life. Both husband and wife are linked to agriculture, the basis of ancient Egyptian life. The death and rebirth of the god, who is referred to as the Green One, is linked to the cycles of the life and death of the land. His wife is the nurturer, the bringer of new life and rebirth. Psychologically, the work examines a new theme for McDermott: unlike the earlier stories that focused directly on the male journey to adulthood, this one examines both the balance between men and women and the conscious and unconscious sides of individuals. *The Voyage of Osiris* is McDermott's first use of watercolors, an appropriate medium as the story deals implicitly with the annual flooding of the Nile. The orange colors of the desert form the background against which the blues and greens of Isis and Osiris interact.

Students in the upper elementary grades can discuss whether or not Osiris, who had spent much time away from home, was partly responsible for the fate that befell him. Noting the importance of his relationship with his wife in the story, they can also discuss the importance of companionship, cooperation, and balance in the myth. The links between the story and the agrarian culture of the people can be traced. Students can study the endpapers, seeing how, moving from left to right, these depict the main characters and events of the story and can use these illustrations as a guide to their own retelling of the myth. If the students are reading a number of McDermott works, they can relate this book to the earlier *Arrow to the Sun* and the later *The Knight of the Lion*, noting similarities and differences in themes, character conflicts, and artistic techniques.

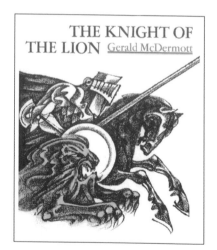

THE KNIGHT OF THE LION
(1979)

Although it deals with a familiar theme, the quest of a young hero to achieve adulthood, *The Knight of the Lion* is unique among McDermott's works. Over eighty pages long, it contains several thousand words of text, and the illustrations are monochromatic. "I deliberately denied myself the use of color, which had been my primary tool for communicating emotions, and used etched line drawings to capture the dark power of the story. The written text was also important to me in suggesting the intense emotions the story held." Based on a French legend written over eight centuries ago, it is the story of Yvain, a self-centered knight who uses his prowess in battle to win the hand of the Lady Laudine. However, in his thoughtlessness, he loses her trust and must make a long and dangerous journey to regain her love. His initial actions have consequences for more than just himself and his lady. Indeed, they result in the devastation of the landscape. The individual's deeds, McDermott is implicitly stating, have repercussions on the social and physical environments through which a character moves. In many ways, Yvain's early reactions are the opposite of those of the Boy in *Arrow to the Sun*, in which a personal quest results in rain reviving the parched desert. Yvain's return journey is a contrast to that found in *The Magic Tree*, in which Mavungu is unable to reverse the consequences of his immature, self-centered actions.

Students in the upper elementary grades may wish to make a large map on which they can place illustrations of the settings, characters, and events of the knight's two journeys. They can discuss how each stage of both journeys reflects elements of his character and why the settings and individuals encountered help to reveal his emotional and spiritual progress or regression. They can also compare the male characters' actions in *Arrow to the Sun* and *The Magic Tree* with those of Yvain.

SUNFLIGHT
(1980)

This well-known legend from pre-Classical Greece illustrates the tragedy that befalls an adolescent who will not heed the wisdom of an older person. Imprisoned in the labyrinth he had created, craftsman Daedalus creates artificial wings for himself and his son, Icarus. As the two begin their flight to freedom, the father warns the boy of the dangers of flying too high or too low. When Icarus recklessly flies toward the sun, the wax holding his wings melts, he plunges into the sea, and he drowns. Daedalus, in many ways, represents the artist who is able to enter the dark world of the unconscious and find a way to return to the light. His art, in this case, the artificial wings, can liberate. Icarus can be seen as the individual who cannot respond to the liberating power of art. King Minos, in contrast to Daedalus, is the person of power who uses his strength to imprison rather than ennoble and free others. "I had visited the Isle of Crete and looked closely at the highly stylized Minoan frescoes and felt that this kind of style best served to communicate the powerful, dark elements of the story. My telling of the story reflects the influence of Joseph Campbell on my thinking. He sparked my interest in the quest of the young person who can't succeed because he is unable to find the middle path."

Like *The Magic Tree*, *Sunflight* employs color to communicate powerful emotions and conflicts. Students in the upper elementary grades can note the dominant background color of each illustration and the emotion it reflects. They can discuss how the changes in color during the course of the book reveal the changing emotions and the movement toward resolutions (positive or negative) of the conflicts. The tragedy depicted on the wordless pages can be narrated by students from the point of view of either the father or the son.

DAUGHTER OF EARTH
A ROMAN MYTH
(1984)

The classical Roman myth of Proserpina, her mother, Ceres, and her husband, Pluto, recounts the origin of the seasonal cycles in a way that reveals the consequences of powerful human emotions. McDermott chose to tell this well-known version of the Greek narrative in order to celebrate the life-giving power of women and the necessity of finding a middle path in life. Ceres links the worlds of above and below and, in the end, creates an uneasy compromise between two patriarchs (Jupiter and Pluto), who try to impose their wills and power arbitrarily. When the daughter of the harvest goddess is abducted by the Lord of the Underworld, the grieving mother withholds her generative powers from the Earth, creating an enduring winter. Only when her daughter returns does spring come to the land. McDermott's illustrations emphasize the differences between the three worlds. Clouds cover the heavens, which are dominated by a stern, scowling Jupiter. The underworld is cramped and crimson colored, controlled by the intense and brooding Pluto. Between these is the world of human beings and of the female goddess whose realm is multicolored and changing. Prosperpina, the daughter, who appears small and girlish in early pictures, reemerges at the conclusion as a woman. McDermott said of the illustrations, "I painted in the style of the ancient Pompeiian frescoes and emulated their color schemes and representational depictions."

Students in the upper elementary grades can notice how the myth links the worlds of the gods with the physical world and human emotions. How do the gods' actions parallel the intense emotional conflicts that are found among human beings, and how does the landscape reflect these relationships? In what ways is this linking between the landscape and emotions similar to that in *The Knight of the Lion* and *The Stonecutter*? Have students compare the early picture of Proserpina picking flowers with that of her emerging from the underworld at the end. How do differences in details, body language, facial expressions, and colors indicate the young woman's increasing maturity? Students may also wish to find out about the symbolic meanings of the flowers she is picking at the beginning.

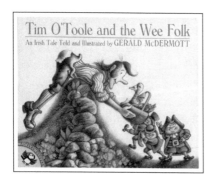

TIM O'TOOLE
AND THE WEE FOLK
AN IRISH TALE
(1990)

The second of McDermott's Irish stories, this one focuses on a character who, the author has noted, "like Coyote and Daniel O'Rourke, is oblivious to the possibilities of life around him." Even though his family is on the edge of starvation, Tim O'Toole must be forced out of the house to find work. The discovery of a group of "wee folk" seems to solve his problems: by demanding that they grant him wishes, he'll both overcome the family's problems and avoid having to work. However, his foolishness causes more problems that only the intervention of the "wee folk" can solve. Although the events are portrayed humorously, the themes are serious. Tim is filled with an unwarranted self-confidence and fails to accept responsibility for the situations in which he finds himself. Without the strength of his wife, who understands both her husband's and her family's problems, a happy resolution would not have been achieved. In adapting this story, McDermott has spoken of his working in a cartoon style and of being inspired by the comic spirit of vaudeville. "Film animators looking at this book would very quickly see that I have been an animator. I think this is most evident in the scene when Tim is climbing down the ladder and the little men are coming out of the hat."

After an initial reading and viewing of the book, students in the middle elementary grades can carefully examine the opening and closing illustrations of Tim and his family at home. How do the differences in colors and details reflect the changes in the family's physical and emotional lives? After this analysis, readers can then consider who is the most responsible for the betterment of the O'Tooles' lives—Tim, his wife, or the wee folk. The role of the wee folk in the "education of the hero" can be compared with the roles of the wee folk in *Daniel O'Rourke* and the crows in *Coyote.*

Bibliographies of Gerald McDermott's Works

BOOKS WRITTEN AND ILLUSTRATED BY GERALD McDERMOTT

Anansi: A Tale from the Ashanti. New York: Henry Holt, 1972.

The Magic Tree: A Tale from the Congo. New York: Henry Holt, 1973.

Arrow to the Sun: A Pueblo Indian Tale. New York: Viking, 1974.

The Stonecutter: A Japanese Folktale. New York: Viking, 1975.

The Voyage of Osiris: A Myth of Ancient Egypt. New York: E. P. Dutton, 1977.

The Knight of the Lion. New York: Four Winds, 1979.

Papagayo the Mischief Maker. New York: E. P. Dutton, 1980.

Sunflight. New York: Four Winds, 1980.

Daughter of Earth: A Roman Myth. New York: Delacorte Press, 1984.

Daniel O'Rourke: An Irish Tale. New York: Viking, 1986.

Adventures in Folklore: Trickster Tales. New Berlin, WI: Jenson Publications, 1989.

The World of Mythology: Gods & Heroes. New Berlin, WI: Jenson Publications, 1989.

Tim O'Toole and the Wee Folk. New York: Viking, 1990.

Zomo the Rabbit: A Trickster Tale from West Africa. San Diego: Harcourt, 1992.

Raven: A Trickster Tale from the Pacific Northwest. San Diego: Harcourt, 1993.

Coyote: A Trickster Tale from the American Southwest. San Diego: Harcourt, 1994.

Musicians of the Sun. New York: Simon and Schuster, 1997.

Jabutí the Tortoise: A Trickster Tale from the Amazon. San Diego: Harcourt, 2001.

Creation. New York: Dutton Books, 2003.

BOOKS ILLUSTRATED BY GERALD McDERMOTT

Carlo Collodi's The Adventures of Pinocchio, translated and adapted by Marianna Mayer. New York: Four Winds, 1981.

Aladdin and the Enchanted Lamp, told by Marianna Mayer. New York: Macmillan, 1985.

The Brambleberrys Animal Alphabet (with Marianna Mayer). Stamford, CT: Longmeadow Press, 1987.

The Brambleberrys Animal Book of Big & Small Shapes (with Marianna Mayer). Stamford, CT: Longmeadow Press, 1987.

The Brambleberrys Animal Book of Colors (with Marianna Mayer). Stamford, CT: Longmeadow Press, 1987.

The Brambleberrys Animal Book of Counting (with Marianna Bayer). Stamford, CT: Longmeadow Press, 1987.

Marcel the Pastry Chef, by Marianna Mayer. New York: Bantam Books, 1991.

FILMS BY GERALD McDERMOTT

The Stonecutter (1960)

Sunflight (1966)

Anansi the Spider (1969)

The Magic Tree (1970)

Arrow to the Sun (1973)

ARTICLES BY GERALD McDERMOTT

"On the Rainbow Trail." *The Horn Book Magazine,* 51 (April 1975): 123–31.

"Caldecott Award Acceptance." *The Horn Book Magazine,* 51 (August 1975): 349–54.

"Sky Father, Earth Mother: An Artist Interprets Myth." *The New Advocate,* 1 (1988): 1–7.

DOCUMENTARY VIDEOS

"COLORES: An Artist's Journey," Albuquerque, NM: KNME, 1995.

"Get to Know Gerald McDermott," San Diego: Harcourt Brace, 1995.

"Dreamweaver," from the series "Wonderful Pages," Columbia, SC: University of South Carolina, 2005.

An Index of Authors, Artists, and Titles

A Story, a Story 18, 19, 60, 61
Aardema, Verna 60, 61, 75, 76
Adventures of Pinocchio, The 5
Akaba, Suekichi 37
Aladdin and the Enchanted Lamp 5
Alexieff, Alexander 2
Ananse's Feast 18, 20, 89, 90
Anansi the Spider: A Tale from the Ashanti
    (book) 4, 6, 13–20, 36, 44, 58, 74
Anansi the Spider (film) 4, 13, 15, 19
Appiah, Peggy 18, 19
Architect of the Moon 44, 46
Arrow to the Sun (book) 4, 6, 11, 21–29,
    33, 44, 50, 52, 67, 74, 82, 83, 92, 100, 101
Arrow to the Sun (film) 3, 4, 28

Begay, Shonto 75, 76
*Bo Rabbit Smart for True: Folktales from the
    Gullah* 60, 61
Borreguita and the Coyote 75, 76
Boy Who Made Dragon Fly, The 75, 76
Bringhurst, Robert 68, 69

Campbell, Joseph 3, 31, 22–23, 28, 101
Carter, Susan 53
Cherry, Lynne 45, 46
Collins, Megan 52, 53
*Coyote: A Trickster Tale from the American
    Southwest* 5, 6, 17, 44, 45, 52, 59, 71–76,
    82, 89, 102, 103
Coyote and the Magic Words 75
Crane Wife, The 36, 37
Creation 5, 6, 77, 91–97
Crow Boy 28, 29
Cushing, Frank 71, 72, 75, 76

Daniel O'Rourke: An Irish Tale 5, 6, 17,
    47–53, 59, 82, 102, 103
Daughter of Earth: A Roman Myth 4, 6, 74,
    82, 83, 102
Dayrell, Elphinstone 18, 19
Dillon, Leo and Diane 61
Dixon, Ann 68, 69

Egielski, Richard 37
Elbl, Martin 45, 46
Eliade, Mircea 4

Fisherman and His Wife, The 36, 37
Flame of Peace, The: A Tale of the Aztecs 82, 83
Frederick 11, 27, 28
Forest, Heather 52, 53

Gal, Laszlo 53
Gilman, Phoebe 36, 37
Glass, Andrew 20, 90
Goble, Paul 96, 97
*Great Kapok Tree, The: A Tale of the Amazon-
    ian Rain Forest* 45, 46
Gypsy Princess, The 36, 37

Haley, Gail 18, 19, 60, 61
Hamilton, Virginia 45, 46, 97
Harris, Christie 68, 69
Harris, Joel Chandler 55
Hero With a Thousand Faces, The 2, 22,
    23–24, 28
Hey, Al 36, 37
Hickox, Rebecca 45, 46
Hillerman, Tony 75, 76
Hodges, Margaret 27, 28
*How Many Spots Does a Leopard Have? And
    Other Tales* 89, 90
*How Rabbit Tricked Otter and Other Cherokee
    Trickster Stories* 60, 61
How Raven Brought Light to the People 68, 69
Howard, Kim 46
Hyman, Trina Schart 28

*In the Beginning: Creation Stories from Around
    the World* 97
In the Night, Still Dark 96, 97

*Jabutí: the Tortoise: A Trickster Tale from the
    Amazon* 5, 6, 17, 44, 45, 52, 59, 74, 82,
    85–90
Jacob, Murv 61
Jaquith, Priscilla 60, 61
Jarrell, Randal 37
Jung, Carl 3, 4, 24
Just a Dream 52, 53
Just So Stories 74, 76

Kiddell-Monroe, Jean 20
Kipling, Rudyard 74, 76

Kitchen Knight, The 27, 28
Knight of the Lion, The 4, 6, 82, 92,
    100–101, 102

Langlois, Henri 2
Lattimore, Deborah Nourse 82, 83
Lee, Jeanne M. 27, 28
Legend of Scarface, The 11, 27, 29
Lent, Blair 19
Lester, Julius 60, 61, 89, 90
Lewis, Richard 96, 97
Lionni, Leo 11, 27, 28

Magic Tree, The: A Tale from the Congo
    (book) 4, 6, 36, 39, 101
Magic Tree, The (film) 3, 4
Mahy, Margaret 18, 20
Ma'ii and Cousin Horned Toad 75, 76
Masks of God, The 3
Mathers, Peter 76
Mayer, Marianna 5
Michelangelo 97
Mollel, Tololwa 18, 20, 45, 46, 89, 90
Momotaro: The Peach Boy 27, 29, 36, 37
Moser, Barry 46, 97
Mouse Woman and the Vanished Princesses
    68, 69
Mufaro's Beautiful Daughters 18, 20
Muller, Robin 52, 53
Musicians of the Sun 5, 6, 27, 52, 68,
    77–83, 92, 94, 96

Neubacher, Gerda 46
Nicholson, George 4
Nightwood, The 52, 53

Papagayo: The Mischief Maker 4, 6, 17,
    39–46, 59, 74
Paterson, Katherine 37
Pinkney, Jerry 61, 90
Promise to the Sun, A 45, 46

Rain Player 82, 83
Rank, Otto 4
Raven: A Trickster Tale from the Pacific
    Northwest 5, 2, 44, 45, 59, 63–69, 73, 74,
    77, 82, 92, 94, 96
Raven's Light: A Myth from the People of the
    Northwest Coast 68, 69
Raven Steals the Light, The 68, 69
Reid, Bill 68, 69
Remaking the Earth: A Creation Story from the
    Great Plains of North America 96, 97

Root, Phyllis 75, 76
Ross, Gayle 60, 61

San Souci, Daniel 29
San Souci, Robert 11, 27, 29
Sendak, Maurice 52, 53
Seven Chinese Brothers, The 18, 20
Shannon, David 90
Sherlock, Philip 18, 20
Shetterly, Robert 68, 69
Shetterly, Susan Hand 68, 69
Shute, Linda 27, 29, 36, 37
Speidel, Sandra 76
Steptoe, John 18, 20
Stonecutter, The: A Japanese Folk Tale (book)
    6, 32–37, 82
Stonecutter, The (film) 1, 3, 32, 34,
    37, 102
Sunflight (book) 6, 36, 52, 82, 89, 101
Sunflight/The Flight of Icarus (film) 3, 4

Tait, Douglas 69
Tales from the Amazon 45, 46
Tales of a Trickster Guinea Pig: Zorro and
    Quwi 45, 46
Tales of an Ashanti Father 18, 19
Tales of Uncle Remus, The: The Adventures of
    Brer Rabbit 60, 61, 89, 90
Tim O'Toole and the Wee Folk 5, 6,
    102–103
Toad is the Uncle of Heaven 27, 28
Tseng, Jean and Mou-sien 20

Van Allsburg, Chris 52, 53
Vidal, Beatriz 46
Voyage of Osiris, The: A Myth of Ancient Egypt
    4, 6, 82, 99–100

Wallace, Ian 44, 46
Watts, James 68, 69
When Birds Could Talk and Bats Could Sing
    45, 46
Where the Wild Things Are 52, 53
Wisniewski, David 82, 83
Who's in Rabbit's House? 60, 61
Why the Sun and Moon Live in the Sky
    18, 19
Willow Maiden, The 52, 53
Winik, T. J. 45, 46
Woman Who Flummoxed the Fairies, The
    52, 53
Wynne-Jones, Tim 44, 46

Yagawa, Sumiko   36, 37
Yashima, Taro   27, 29
Yorinks, Arthur   36, 37
Young, Ed   61, 97

Zemach, Margo   36, 37
*Zomo the Rabbit: A Trickster Tale from West
   Africa*   5, 6, 55–61, 73
Zuni Folktales   75, 76

About the Author

JON C. STOTT is Professor Emeritus Children's Literature, University of Alberta, Canada. Dr. Stott is a long time friend and student of Gerald McDermott's work.